"A new believer needs the church  ...n and service. In *Ten Essentials for Ne...* ...le guide to help new believers in th... ...n-focused resource is a must for ch... ...u disciple people."

—**Ed Stetzer**, PhD, dean, Talbot School of Theology

"Have you recently become a Christian? Or are you trying to help new believers grow? Then this book is for you. It helpfully clarifies key truths, warmly encourages you to grow in your faith, and honestly addresses questions you may have been afraid to ask."

—**Christopher W. Morgan**, dean and professor of theology, California Baptist University; author/editor of more than 25 books

"*Ten Essentials for New Christians* is hardly just another 'essentials of the faith' book. Instead, Stan and Bruce offer us an outlook where everything is steeped in the incomprehensible love God has for us. Their book is timely in an era where being right tragically outpaces showing love. I cannot recommend this book enough."

—**Bryan Loritts**, teaching pastor, The Summit Church, NC; author, *The Offensive Church*

"The essence of the Christian faith is God's love expressed through Jesus. Stan and Bruce invite new believers to allow God's love to transform their hearts and impact every aspect of their lives. This book will help you find life in Jesus, love your neighbors, and help others to do the same."

—**Kevin A. Thompson**, married life pastor at Bayside Church, CA

TEN ESSENTIALS FOR NEW CHRISTIANS

Stan Jantz
and
Bruce Bickel

HARVEST HOUSE PUBLISHERS
EUGENE, OREGON

Cover design by Brock Book Design Co., Charles Brock

Cover image © Ismael / Adobe Stock

Interior design by Matt Shoemaker Design

For bulk, special sales, or ministry purchases, please call 1-800-547-8979.
Email: CustomerService@hhpbooks.com

Ten Essentials for New Christians
Copyright © 2024 by Stan Jantz and Bruce Bickel
Published by Harvest House Publishers
Eugene, Oregon 97408
www.harvesthousepublishers.com

ISBN 978-0-7369-8812-4 (pbk)
ISBN 978-0-7369-8813-1 (eBook)

Library of Congress Control Number: 2023938671

Printed in the United States of America

23 24 25 26 27 28 29 30 31 32 / BP / 10 9 8 7 6 5 4 3 2 1

Contents

An Essential Comment About Christian Essentials

Congratulations! You have made the most important decision you will ever make. You have decided to say yes to Jesus. You have responded to his invitation to have a relationship with him that will profoundly impact your life, both now and forever. Whether you made that decision recently or some time ago, the question you are most likely asking is, "What's next?" It's one thing to say yes to Jesus, and quite another to follow him.

That's what this book is all about. Our goal is to help you determine the next steps in your Christian life so your relationship with Jesus pleases him and makes a difference in your life, not to mention the lives of others. The steps you will be taking are really very easy to grasp, but sometimes difficult to take. That's because the things Jesus is asking you to do don't always come naturally, which means you will need to be intentional about your life as a new Christian.

From now on, your life will be defined by and driven by love. According to Jesus, loving God and loving others is your top priority—not just now but for the rest of your life. It won't always be easy to carry out this "great commandment," but it will be infinitely rewarding. By living your life by faith, you will realize the love God has for you, you will embark on the adventure of loving God, and you will discover the joy of loving others.

We've divided this book into three parts, all based on these love principles. Woven into those three parts are the essentials we have found to be helpful for new Christians. We have devoted one chapter to each of the ten essentials. Truthfully, they are essential for every Christian, no matter how long they have followed Jesus. Each chapter ends with our concluding thought about the essential under discussion, and our answer (which is by no means definitive) to a commonly asked question on the topic.

By orienting your life around the power of love, you will be drawn ever closer to the heart of God. That's because above all else, God is love. May this reality take root in your life as you grow in the love of God and increase in your love for others. As you experience this book, come back to this page from time to time to review what it means to love and be loved by God:

> God showed how much he loved us by sending his one and only Son into the world so that we might have eternal life through him. This is real love—not that we loved God, but that he loved us and sent his Son as a sacrifice to take away our sins.
>
> Dear friends, since God loved us that much, we surely ought to love each other. No one has ever seen God. But if we love each other, God lives in us, and his love is brought to full expression in us (1 John 4:9-12).

Part One

Realize the Limitless Love God Has for You

Chapter 1
God Made You for Something Special

As you begin your journey with Jesus, we're going to start with you, not because you are the most important person in God's story (that would be Jesus, in case you're wondering), but because God loves you so much that he sent his only Son to die for you so you could (1) have eternal life, and (2) do something special for him.

If that thought causes you to stop and wonder why God would think so highly of you, don't worry. You're not alone. The great poet King David pondered the questions of "Why me?" and "Why us?" in this famous psalm:

> When I look at the night sky and see the work of your fingers—
> the moon and the stars you set in place—
> what are mere mortals that you should think about them,
> human beings that you should care for them?
> Yet you made them only a little lower than God
> and crowned them with glory and honor.
> (Psalm 8:3-5)

The reason for God's extraordinary love comes from his nature. God is defined by love (1 John 4:16). He can't help but love you, and there's nothing that can separate you from his love (Romans 8:38-39). But God also loves you because he made you for something special. You aren't on this earth by accident or random chance. You were created by God in his very image. Here's how the Bible describes this incredible creative act. Notice the word *us* in this verse. It means all three Persons of the Trinity—Father, Son, and Holy Spirit—were involved in the creation of humankind:

> Then God said, "Let us make human beings in our image, to be like us" (Genesis 1:26).

Made in God's Image

Think about that for a minute. You and every other person born on this earth bear the image, or imprint, of God. You don't *look* like God because God is a spirit. But you have some of the same character qualities God has:

- You have a heart with the emotions of love, care, and compassion.
- You have a mind that can think and plan and dream.
- You have a will that allows you to choose and make decisions.

And there's something else you have because you are made in God's image. You are immortal. That doesn't mean you have always existed. Only God is eternal. Your immortality means you are made in God's image and will live forever. This awesome reality inspired C.S. Lewis to write this about us and others we encounter in life:

There are no ordinary people. You have never talked to a mere mortal. Nations, cultures, arts, civilizations—these are mortal, and their life is to ours as the life of a gnat. But it is immortals whom we joke with, work with, marry, snub and exploit—immortal horrors or everlasting splendors.[1]

When We Ruined Everything

Imagine yourself in the Garden of Eden, that perfect place God created for his image bearers to live. You're immortal, you walk and talk with God, and you have an adoring spouse—not to mention you know all the animals by name. But for some reason, that's not enough.

You have the run of the Garden except for "the tree of the knowledge of good and evil." God is very clear that you should not eat the fruit from this tree, for if you do, "you are sure to die" (Genesis 2:17). But that's exactly what you do. Oh, you try to place the blame on the other person (if you're Adam) or on the serpent (if you're Eve), but the deed is done. You have willfully disobeyed the one warning God gave you. And the penalty, as God promised, is death.

"But wait a minute," you may protest, "that wasn't me in the Garden." You're right; it was Adam and Eve. But as the representatives of the human race God made, their sin infected everyone born after them like a virus passed on by human contact. The only difference is that sin is a virus passed on by human nature.

But God's Love Is So Great

We're going to talk about God's solution for our sin problem in the next chapter. In this chapter we want to focus on a single idea: God made you for something special. Despite the sin nature that every person born since Adam and Eve has inherited, God's love is so great that he saved you while you were still lost in your sin:

> God showed his great love for us by sending Christ
> to die for us while we were still sinners (Romans 5:8).

Never forget this incredible reality: God made you, saved you, and has plans for you, both now and in the future.

You Are God's Masterpiece

We live in a time of great anxiety. Because of circumstances pretty much outside our control, the world presents us with challenges that can make even the most confident person question their worth. Perhaps you feel that way. You may wonder if you're good enough, smart enough, or privileged enough to be a success—at least by the standards of the world.

Stop thinking that way. We're here to tell you that you are already a success in God's eyes. You were made in his image, you have been redeemed by his Son, you are indwelled by the Holy Spirit, and you have been designed by God to do something special. The reason we know this to be true is that the Bible tells us:

> God saved you by his grace when you believed. And
> you can't take credit for this; it is a gift from God.
> Salvation is not a reward for the good things we have
> done, so none of us can boast about it. For we are
> God's masterpiece. He has created us anew in Christ
> Jesus, so we can do the good things he planned for
> us long ago (Ephesians 2:8-10).

Notice the word *masterpiece*. When an artist creates a masterpiece, whether a painting or a piece of music or a book, it refers to his or her crowning achievement. That's what you are to God. Of all the beautiful things he created, including the universe itself, you are his crowning achievement. But it doesn't stop there. God didn't create you to sit on the sidelines. He created you and gave you new life in Jesus *so that you could do the good things he planned for you long ago.*

How to Get Good at Doing Good Things

We're going to give it to you straight. As a Christian beginning your life with Jesus, you don't have a choice. You can't sit passively on the sidelines, reluctant to get involved in worthwhile activities. It's your responsibility and your privilege as a new Christian to get good at doing good things. It's not easy, but it's pretty simple.

The first thing you can do is to discover the spiritual gifts God has given you through the Holy Spirit. In addition, there are some excellent assessment tools to help you identify your natural character traits and abilities. The more you know what you are good at, the more effective you will be in your service to God and others.

Once you have a realistic understanding of your spiritual as well as your natural gifts, there are three strategies that will maximize your gifts and abilities so you can give God your best as you do the good things he has planned for you to do.

Put in the Time

The most common way to get good at something is to spend the time needed to become good. World-class athletes don't rely on natural abilities alone. They "put in the time" to achieve a high level of skill and effectiveness. Same goes for artists, teachers, pastors, nonprofit leaders, and business professionals. And here's a little secret: Just because you are passionate about something doesn't mean you are good at it.

Mark Cuban, billionaire owner of the Dallas Mavericks and *Shark Tank* star, had several passions growing up, but he didn't follow any of them because he wasn't any good at any of the things he was passionate about. Instead, Cuban pursued what he was good at, and he worked hard to get better. "If you put in enough time, and you get really good," says Cuban, "I will give you a little secret: Nobody quits anything they are good at because it's fun to be good. It's fun to be one of the best."

Bestselling author Mark Batterson put in the time and effort to gain the skill he needed to write. Before he even attempted to write his first book, Batterson spent two years reading hundreds of books. Through his reading, practice, and study, Batterson developed the skill to be a good writer and, consequently, a bestselling author. And now he is passionate about writing and the power of books to change lives.

Find a Mentor

Mentorship is a powerful and effective way to acquire skill in service to God. A mentor is simply a wise and trusted counselor or teacher. Both of us have been proactive about seeking and learning from mentors who have taught us by their words and demonstrated through their lives how to be effective in work and ministry. There are many examples of mentorship in the Bible.

- Jethro mentored his son-in-law Moses (Exodus 18:13-27).
- Elijah mentored Elisha (1 Kings 19:15-21).

- Paul mentored Timothy (1 Corinthians 4:17).
- And most famously, Jesus mentored his disciples (Mark 3:13-19).

Seek Wisdom

There's one more way to get good at something, and this may be the most powerful pathway of them all. It's a way suggested by the Bible in the book of Exodus. There you will find the fascinating story of Bezalel, a Jewish craftsman who was assigned by God to design and make beautiful artifacts for the tabernacle. Here's how Moses, who wrote the book of Exodus, describes the process God used to give skill to Bezalel:

> Then the LORD said to Moses, "See, I have chosen Bezalel, son of Uri, the son of Hur, of the tribe of Judah, and I have filled him with the Spirit of God, with wisdom, with understanding, with knowledge and with all kinds of skills—to make artistic designs for work in gold, silver and bronze, to cut and set stones, to work in wood, and to engage in all kinds of crafts" (Exodus 31:1-5 NIV).

The key word in this passage is *wisdom,* which is equivalent to the word *skill.* In fact, to live with wisdom means you are living with skill. Proverbs 4:7 (NIV) says: "The beginning of wisdom is this: Get wisdom." And how do you get wisdom? The answer is found in James 1:5 (NIV): "If any of you lacks wisdom, you should ask God, who gives generously to all without finding fault, and it will be given to you."

Just Do It

As God's masterpiece, created anew in Christ Jesus so you can do those things he planned for you long ago, you have a responsibility and a privilege to just do it, whatever it is God is calling you to do. Once you find what you were made to do, you will know it's right because you will accomplish things you never knew you were capable of doing. You just need to put in the time, find someone to mentor you, and seek wisdom. Just do it and you will be amazed at the results.

AN ESSENTIAL FOR NEW CHRISTIANS

Realize that God loves you just the way you are, but also that God loves you too much to let you stay the way you are. You see, God has a goal for you, and it's not for you to be the best version of yourself. He wants you to be like Jesus (Romans 8:29). In return, you will show God that you love him by doing those things Jesus commands you to do (John 14:15). Make a commitment to diligently explore the depths of God's love for you. It will change your image of God and your image of yourself.

Q&A
HOW CAN I KNOW GOD'S WILL FOR MY LIFE?

Anyone who is following Jesus should want to do his will. Living the Christian life is a journey, and the specific paths that journey is going to take aren't clearly marked. You know your final destination, but you don't always know what lies around the next bend. Here are four things you can do to better discern God's will, whether it's for a short assignment or a career change. But ultimately you need to trust God by faith to lead you where he wants you to go.

- *Pray about it.* Ask God to lead you along the right path and to give you his peace that you're doing the right thing.
- *Stay focused on God's Word.* You probably won't find specific verses that will tell you what to do, but allow the Holy Spirit to speak to you and give you wisdom.
- *Seek the wise counsel of mature believers* who know you well. You can trust the perception and advice of others who love you and care about you. It's ultimately your decision, but "there is safety in having many advisers" (Proverbs 11:14).
- *Do your homework.* God gave you intelligence. Use it. Whatever it is you are considering, take advantage of the resources to help you make a wise decision.

Here's something else we've learned about God's will over the years: God's will is a circle rather than a dot. What we mean is that there may not be one specific thing God wants you to do; rather, you may be presented with more than one path that pleases him. If you follow the steps outlined above, it may end up that you have multiple options, all of which could have positive results. Trust God to guide you and then use your own judgment to make decisions—as long as your judgment is based on your growing relationship with God.

Chapter 2

Jesus Died So You Could Live

You can't understand Jesus unless you understand humanity's need for a Savior, so we begin this chapter with a quick review:

Q: *Why do we need a Savior?*

A: Because humanity is infected with a sin virus that separates us from God and is punishable by eternal death.

Q: *What is God's rescue plan for us?*

A: Jesus is our salvation.

The reason you said yes to Jesus was to receive his offer of salvation. So, we begin with a condensed version of Jesus' biography, and follow that with a longer discussion of the eternal salvation you have received through him.

Jesus: Born to Die

You know the story: Jesus, a child conceived out of wedlock, was born to Mary (who became pregnant by the intervention of the Holy Spirit) and to her fiancé Joseph while they were visiting Bethlehem. No room at the Bethlehem B&B, so a stable was turned into a makeshift birthing room, with all the sounds and smells that accompany livestock—rather ignominious and inconspicuous surroundings for the nighttime birth of God's Son.

Most people have a plastic nativity set that they fetch from the attic once a year. But the fondness for this beloved scene of baby Jesus in a manger usually distracts people from one of the most perplexing questions of all time: How can Jesus be both God and human at the same time?

Was Jesus Human or Was He God?

He was both. Known as "the incarnation," Jesus, being fully God, came to earth as fully human. Except for the sin nature of every human, Jesus was as human as possible. With Mary as his mother and God as his father, he wasn't entirely identical to us, but he can identify with us. (It seems impossible to understand for all of us who lack the intelligence of God. But like the concept of the Trinity, Christians have faith in the truth of the incarnation without fully comprehending how it works.)

The incarnation is an important tenet of the Christian faith. If we deny the deity of Jesus, then his death was not sufficient to serve as a sacrifice for the sins of humanity. If we deny his human nature, then we minimize the pain and agony he endured on the cross. But he was both, which means that Christians have a Savior (because he was God) who is able to sympathize with our struggles and tragedies on earth (because he was human).

> So then, since we have a great High Priest who has entered heaven, Jesus the Son of God, let us hold firmly to what we believe. This High Priest of ours understands our weaknesses, for he faced all of the same testings we do, yet he did not sin. So let us come boldly to the throne of our gracious God.

There we will receive his mercy, and we will find grace
to help us when we need it most (Hebrews 4:15-16).

The Miracles of Jesus: Proof He Was God

Jesus emerged from relative obscurity at about the age of 30. He
quickly created a buzz about being the Messiah by performing supernatural miracles:

- Healing the sick
- Restoring sight to the blind
- Healing the lame
- Casting out demons
- Raising the dead back to life

Sometimes the miracles were performed within an intimate group
of a few people. Other times, there were bigger audiences, such as
when Jesus supernaturally multiplied a boy's sack lunch (of five bar-
ley biscuits and two dried fish sticks) into sufficient quantity to feed
more than 5,000 men, plus the women and children who accompanied
them. Bible scholars estimate there were in the range of 15,000 to
20,000 eyewitnesses to this miracle. There are over 30 miracles of Jesus
reported in the Bible, but we'll move on because we assume that you
aren't skeptical about the well-documented supernatural evidence that
proved he was God.

The Message of Jesus: It Isn't What You Do but Who You Know

While his *miracles* made Jesus *famous* with the common folks, his
message made him *infamous* with the religious elite. In particular, Jesus

confronted the Pharisees (the strictest sect in Judaism) because of their screwed-up "how to get to heaven" theology. Over the span of three years, Jesus emphasized these two principles:

First, salvation is not based on a checklist of dos and don'ts. Jesus told the Pharisees they were so self-absorbed that they had little love for God. The pretentious and sanctimonious Jewish Pharisees had advertised themselves as being favored by God because they excelled at following religious rituals. They did a great job of making the commoners believe that God loved the Pharisees more than he loved everyone else because Pharisees strictly adhered to all of God's laws. Jesus knew that the only thing they truly loved was their position of power and prestige. The Pharisees missed the lesson of the Ten Commandments: No amount of rule-keeping would make anyone good enough to get eternal life with a holy God. God grades on a pass/fail basis, and everyone fails.

Second, to get to God, you have to go through Jesus. Jesus identified himself as the Son of God and said that the only way for anyone to reach God was to go through him. Jesus said it simply and succinctly:

> Jesus told him, "I am the way, the truth, and the life. No one can come to the Father except through me" (John 14:6).

Bottom line, Jesus was saying this: No one is good enough to get to heaven on their own efforts, but he could pay the price for their sin that deserves hell. God's forgiveness, grace, and mercy are available through him, and no one is so bad that they can't be rescued by his love.

The Mission of Jesus: Salvation by the Cross and the Resurrection

The message of Jesus—that he alone can bring salvation to members of the human race—was accomplished by his death on the cross (as a sacrifice for our sins) and proven by his resurrection three days later (displaying his power over death). But you might be wondering about two questions:

First, why did Jesus have to die? If there was no sacrificial death, there could be no salvation for us. Christ's death on behalf of a sinful humanity is called substitutionary atonement. Crucifixion of the innocent Jesus was the reparation for the sins of humanity. Christ's undeserved death was substituted in place of the death we deserved. He paid our penalty with his life.

> God presented Jesus as the sacrifice for sin. People are made right with God when they believe that Jesus sacrificed his life, shedding his blood (Romans 3:25a).

Second, what is so important about the resurrection? Here are a few of the many reasons why Christ's resurrection from the dead is important in the Christian faith.

- It proves God's power over death and the other laws of nature.
- It validates why God deserves our honor and worship.

- It acknowledges God's sovereignty over life in general, and our individual lives specifically.
- It fulfilled Old Testament prophecies from previous centuries giving credence to the reliability of the Bible.

Salvation: The High Cost of a Free Gift

Since the first century, Christians have been using the term *gospel* to refer to the good news that Christ's sacrifice brings salvation to us. It is used more than 75 times in the New Testament. Translated from the Greek, it literally means (you guessed it) "Good News."

Don't miss the key component in this plan: God's salvation is offered to us as a *free* gift. It is totally "come as you are" to God, regardless of your sins and shady past. You don't have to clean up your act first as a prerequisite for gaining access to God. God forgives your sins—past, present, and future—by accepting the blood of his crucified Son as a sufficient sacrifice. On this basis, God declares you are righteous and establishes an intimate, eternal relationship with you.

> So we praise God for the glorious grace he has poured out on us who belong to his dear Son. He is so rich in kindness and grace that he purchased our freedom with the blood of his Son and forgave our sins (Ephesians 1:6-7).

That is how much God loves you. So much that he was willing to sacrifice his Son on the cross to pay the ransom for your salvation. Never forget that the salvation that cost you nothing was paid for with the priceless blood of Jesus on the cross.

Salvation: How Does It Work?

While the Pharisees, as a group, hated Jesus, at least one of their members was genuinely intrigued by the message Jesus preached. His name was Nicodemus, and he arranged a clandestine, nighttime meeting with Jesus, looking for an explanation of how to get into the Kingdom of Heaven. Here's how the conversation went:

> *Jesus:* "I tell you the truth, unless you are born again, you cannot see the Kingdom of God."
>
> *Nicodemus*: "What do you mean? How can an old man go back into his mother's womb and be born again?"
>
> *Jesus*: "I assure you, no one can enter the Kingdom of God without being born of water and the Spirit. Humans can reproduce only human life, but the Holy Spirit gives birth to spiritual life. So don't be surprised when I say, 'You must be born again'" (John 3:3-7).

Being "born again" is a phrase often used by Christians to explain their status of receiving God's free gift of salvation (interchangeable with being "saved"). Nicodemus wasn't thinking beyond the dimension of human life on earth. He missed the point that Jesus was speaking of rebirth of a spiritual dimension. The apostle Paul said it this way:

> This means that anyone who belongs to Christ has become a new person. The old life is gone; a new life has begun! (2 Corinthians 5:17).

Salvation gives us a spiritual overhaul. The old sinful human nature that came at birth dies and is replaced with a new spiritual nature that is Christlike. It is instantaneous in some respects and progressive in other respects.

At the moment of your salvation, God declared you justified. *Justification* is what happens when God declares that you are righteous (sin free) because the penalty for your sin is considered paid by Christ's death. Just as an accountant will "justify the books" when a debt has been paid, your sin debt is satisfied by Christ. You are justified, once and for all. That's exactly how God sees you—just as if you had never sinned.

But every Christian continues to sin after salvation. God is not unrealistic in his expectations. While it is his will that we live a sinless, Christlike life after our salvation, he knows we are still encumbered by our old nature. Because God wants us to be sanctified (meaning holy and suitable for his purposes), he infuses us with the Holy Spirit at the moment of our salvation so we can experience spiritual growth. This process of *sanctification* continues for the remainder of our physical lifetime. Hopefully our spiritual journey has us sinning less and less as we become more and more spiritually mature.

Salvation: What Does It Mean to "Accept Jesus as Your Personal Savior"?

Many Christians explain their salvation with this simple statement: "I accepted Jesus as my personal Savior." This expression is used so often that you might think these exact words are in the Bible. They aren't. This phrase is accurate, but it can be misleading unless you have a correct understanding of the meaning behind it.

Accepting Jesus: The Meaning Behind the Words

Sometimes the word *accept* conveys a passive, docile, and indifferent situation (like when you accept bad news or accept the fact you're getting older). But *accepting* Jesus is serious business. When new believers *accept* Jesus, they are acknowledging that Jesus is God, repenting of their sins and receiving Christ's forgiveness, and declaring their allegiance to Christ as their Lord and Savior.

Repentance: Much More Than Just Being Sorry

While salvation is offered to all, it is obtained only by those whose response is grounded in repentance. Jesus made this very clear when he said that his purpose in coming to earth was to bring salvation to those who are repentant for their sins:

> "I have come to call not those who think they are
> righteous, but those who know they are sinners and
> need to repent" (Luke 5:32).

In the parlance of the Bible, repentance goes far beyond a cursory "I'm sorry." Biblical repentance conveys that you intend to:

Change your direction. You will stop going the way you have been headed; you will make a U-turn and head in a new direction. This is not merely figurative. Sometimes your repentance at salvation actually means you are going to refrain from going to certain places you know are not spiritually healthy for you.

Reform your behavior. You are going to stop doing certain things; you will establish new habits.

Recalibrate your motivation. At the core, being a Christian is not about behavior modification and sin management. Your relationship with Christ is the essence of your salvation. As you grow in your understanding of God's grace, love, and commitment to you, your motivation will be to respond with thoughts and conduct that reflect your love and respect for him.

Commence the celebration. Your sins—past, present, and future—are forgiven when you accept Christ. Although you will prove to be a repeat offender, confessed sin should carry with it no guilt or shame. Jesus does not love you less because of your past sins, and he won't love you less when you sin again. He celebrates the restoration of his relationship with you that happens with your repentance. Don't let Satan shame you into hiding from Jesus in self-reproach. God is eager to embrace you as a loving father.

Faith and Belief: Total Reliance on the Only One Who Can Save You

A repentant attitude includes the humility and realization that Jesus is the only one who can save you. Our best efforts, compared to a holy God, are less impressive than filthy rags (Isaiah 64:6). Furthermore, unless you believe that Jesus Christ is God and that he alone is capable of determining your eternal destiny, you will be reticent to surrender control of your life to him. You need complete faith in the saving power of Jesus; without it, you will approach God's offer of salvation half-heartedly, with hesitation, and with dubious commitment.

Jesus wants more than just a sterile mental belief in his existence. Big deal. Even Satan and his demons believe that God exists (James 2:19). God also wants you to have an emotional and visceral faith in him that is rooted in your heart. This is the type of faith that drives you to commitment and action.

Therefore, since we have been made right in God's
sight by faith, we have peace with God because of
what Jesus Christ our Lord has done for us (Romans
5:1).

Personal Savior: When Following Christ Becomes a Relationship Instead of a Religion

Most religions in the world emphasize human efforts that are necessary to reach an aloof and impersonal deity. Christianity is the only faith that emphasizes God's sacrifice to reach down to rescue humanity. God's offer of salvation is extended to each of us, individually. It is not "personal" in the sense that it is offered to you and you alone. But it is very personal in the sense that he invites you into an intimate, one-to-one relationship for your earthly lifetime and beyond.

The role of Jesus as "Savior" refers to the fact that he offers to save you from the death penalty for your sins. That's his part. Duh! But what about the part of the new believer? Like the natural reaction of a criminal toward the governor who has just entered a pardon and turned off the switch to the electric chair, new believers approach "accepting Jesus as our personal Savior" with an even deeper sense of love and gratitude for the mercy shown to us.

The Bible doesn't present a specific formula for accepting God's gift of salvation. There is no prescribed script. But in a famous sermon (the "Sermon on the Mount" in Matthew 5), Jesus describes the attitudes and frame of mind of the believer who will enter the Kingdom of Heaven. The new believer who approaches Jesus to accept him as personal Lord and Savior is one who:

TEN ESSENTIALS FOR NEW CHRISTIANS

- acknowledges being spiritually bankrupt and recognizes a need for God and the fact that they have nothing to offer him (verse 3);
- regrets and mourns over their sin and the disconnection from God caused by that sin (verse 4);
- approaches God in humility, having no presumption that God owes them anything or that they have done anything to merit God's mercy (verse 5);
- has a hunger and thirst for God's righteousness (verse 6);
- is inclined to show mercy to others because they are respectful of the mercy God has extended to them (verse 7);
- endeavors to live a God-honoring life not because it is mandated but from a heartfelt motivation (verse 8);
- seeks to bring God's peace to others despite the self-sacrifice required in the effort (verse 9); and
- claims the name of Christ in the face of persecution, knowing that his way is true and right (verse 10).

That is a lot of theology. Few people comprehend all of it when they come to Christ. None of us should be intimidated by it. We can find encouragement by the thief who was hanging on the cross next to Christ. He didn't know any theology, and all he said was, "Jesus, remember me when you come into your Kingdom." Jesus heard what the thief said. More importantly, Jesus knew the thief's heart and responded: "I assure you, today you will be with me in paradise" (Luke

23:42-43). That thief's utterance was a sufficient and effective "I accept you as my personal Savior" prayer.

AN ESSENTIAL FOR NEW CHRISTIANS

Love is the reason God sent Jesus into the world to give his life for us so that we might be rescued from our sinful condition and our rebellion against God and be restored to a right relationship with him.

> God showed his great love for us by sending Christ to die for us while we were still sinners (Romans 5:8).

The greatest thought you could ever have is this: God put this incredible plan into action because of you. He loves you that much. Live in constant appreciation for the salvation you have received, knowing that the price for your sins was paid by Christ taking your place on the cross. Jesus suffered death so you can have eternal life that you didn't deserve.

Q&A
DOES JESUS SAVE EVERYONE?

Jesus said that the short answer is no, absolutely not. Not everyone is saved.

To our human sensitivities, this answer seems harsh. But remember that God "does not want anyone to be destroyed but wants everyone to repent" (2 Peter 3:9). His design is that "everyone who believes in him will not perish but have eternal life" (John 3:16). So, some are saved because they believe in Jesus, and others are not saved because they have chosen to reject Christ. As Jesus said:

> "You can enter God's Kingdom only through the narrow gate [meaning Jesus]. The highway to hell is broad, and its gate is wide for the many who choose that way. But the gateway to life is very narrow and the road is difficult, and only a few ever find it" (Matthew 7:13-14).

Jesus cautioned that some people on the wide road—living for themselves—mistakenly believe that their token acknowledgment of Jesus is enough to get them through the "narrow gate." Using the illustration of sheep (those who are saved) and goats (the unsaved), Jesus gave this warning about the Day of Judgment:

> "All the nations will be gathered in [God's] presence, and he will separate the people as a shepherd separates the sheep from the goats. He will place the sheep at his right hand and the goats at his left.

"Then the King will say to those on his right [the sheep], 'Come, you who are blessed by my Father, inherit the Kingdom prepared for you from the creation of the world. For I was hungry, and you fed me. I was thirsty, and you gave me a drink. I was a stranger, and you invited me into your home. I was naked, and you gave me clothing. I was sick, and you cared for me. I was in prison, and you visited me.'...

"Then the King will turn to those on the left [the goats] and say, 'Away with you, you cursed ones, into the eternal fire prepared for the devil and his demons. For I was hungry, and you didn't feed me. I was thirsty, and you didn't give me a drink. I was a stranger, and you didn't invite me into your home. I was naked, and you didn't give me clothing. I was sick and in prison, and you didn't visit me.'

"Then they will reply, 'Lord, when did we ever see you hungry or thirsty or a stranger or naked or sick or in prison, and not help you?'

"And he will answer, 'I tell you the truth, when you refused to help the least of these my brothers and sisters, you were refusing to help me.'

"And they will go away into eternal punishment, but the righteous will go into eternal life" (Matthew 25:31-46).

Notice that the goats (the unsaved) are shocked that the King does not consider them to be sheep (the saved). The King explains that the goats did not care for the poor, but we know that God doesn't give tickets to heaven simply for doing good deeds. ("God saved you by his grace when you believed…Salvation is not a reward for the good things we have done"—Ephesians 2:8-9.) What distinguishes the sheep from the goats is not their actions but their attitudes:

As the true sheep followed Jesus, they lived unselfishly for him and others. They spent their time, energy, and resources in kindness and caring for those who couldn't care for themselves. They acted with humility. The intentions of their hearts were aligned with the character of the King.

In contrast, the goats lived for themselves. The King found no evidence that they spent their time, energy, and resources on anyone other than themselves. They were selfish and uncaring. Their intentions were in direct opposition with the character of the King.

Jesus saves everyone who comes to him in repentance and in genuine submission. These attitudes need to be in the heart of every sinner seeking salvation. It is not enough to be a goat who says, "I love you, Jesus." The King will say, "You don't truly love Jesus unless you love like Jesus." Jesus saves those who come to him with the desire to be fully devoted to him. The goats say they love Jesus, but they never left the carnal ease of the wide road. They miss out on salvation because they:

- like the idea of salvation but resist the concept of submission;
- want the rewards of salvation without assuming any responsibilities for service to Christ;
- claim some connection with Jesus but don't want to be inconvenienced by him; and

- love the idea of forgiveness from God but have no intention of making a lifelong commitment to Jesus.

The Bible is clear about this. Those who come to Jesus in true repentance, humility, and genuine commitment are saved. Those who approach Jesus half-heartedly and insist on their own terms are "goats" who are walking on the wide path toward the wide gate that leads to hell.

Chapter 3

The Holy Spirit Is Jesus in You

We have already quoted John 3:16, the most famous verse in the Bible (you can never quote this verse too many times):

> "This is how God loved the world: He gave his one and only Son, so that everyone who believes in him will not perish but have eternal life."

This life-giving statement is part of a larger conversation Jesus had with Nicodemus (whom you met in chapter 2) that includes information about the Holy Spirit, the third person in the Trinity along with God the Father and Jesus the Son. (If you want to skip to the question at the end of this chapter about the Trinity, go ahead and do that now. We'll wait for you.)

We quoted the full conversation between Jesus and Nicodemus in the last chapter. Here is the part where Jesus describes the Holy Spirit to Nicodemus:

> "Humans can reproduce only human life, but the Holy Spirit gives birth to spiritual life. So don't be surprised when I say, 'You must be born again.' The wind blows wherever it wants. Just as you can hear

> the wind but can't tell where it comes from or where
> it is going, so you can't explain how people are born
> of the Spirit" (John 3:6-8).

The use of *wind* to describe the Holy Spirit is so important. When you were born, a sure sign that you were alive was when you took your first breath. In a spiritual sense, the same thing happened when you were born again. You became alive in Jesus Christ because you breathed in the wind or life-giving power of the Holy Spirit. Without the Holy Spirit in your life, you are spiritually dead. But with him, you have new life from heaven.

Who Is the Holy Spirit?

The Holy Spirit is often misunderstood by Christians. Some see him as a mysterious, impersonal force. Others think he can be used at will for their own advantage. And some ignore the Holy Spirit altogether because they associate him with churches that seem to get overly emotional and sometimes speak in tongues. We want to dispel these misunderstandings by giving you three characteristics of the Holy Spirit.

The Holy Spirit Is a Person

The first thing to know is that the Holy Spirit is as much a person as God and Jesus. All three share the same character and qualities. Yet the three persons of the Trinity have unique and distinct roles. Notice the way Jesus refers to the Holy Spirit as a unique person, separate from himself and his Father:

> "When the Father sends the Advocate as my repre-
> sentative—that is, the Holy Spirit—he will teach

you everything and will remind you of everything
I have told you" (John 14:26).

Here are some qualities of the Holy Spirit that only a *person* could
have:

- He has a mind (Romans 8:27).
- He loves (Romans 15:30).
- He knows the things of God (1 Corinthians 2:10-11).
- He teaches us (1 Corinthians 2:13).
- He can be offended (Ephesians 4:30).

The Holy Spirit Is a Promise

On the night he was betrayed, Jesus met with his disciples for a
meal. The Gospel of John devotes five chapters to this dramatic evening,
showing how important it was for the followers of Jesus then and now.
Throughout their time together, Jesus gave instructions on a variety of
topics, including a "new commandment" that they love each other in
the same way that Jesus loved them. In fact, this love for one another
would "prove to the world" that they were true followers of Jesus (John
13:34-35). Jesus also made several promises to his disciples:

- He was going to prepare a place in heaven for them (John 14:2).
- He would return to get them so they would always be with him (John 14:3, 28).
- He was leaving them with the gift of "peace of mind and heart" so they wouldn't be troubled or afraid (John 14:27).

- The people of the world would hate them because they belong to Jesus (John 15:18-21).
- God the Father would send the Holy Spirit (John 14:16-17).

To emphasize the importance of his promise that the Holy Spirit would come, Jesus talked about the Holy Spirit five times during his evening conversation with his disciples. Notice how Jesus describes the Holy Spirit as our "Advocate." This means the Holy Spirit is supporting you, pleading for you, acting as your intercessor:

> "I will ask the Father, and he will give you another Advocate, who will never leave you. He is the Holy Spirit, who leads into all truth. The world cannot receive him, because it isn't looking for him and doesn't recognize him. But you know him, because he lives with you now and later will be in you" (John 14:16-17).

> "When the Father sends the Advocate as my representative—that is, the Holy Spirit—he will teach you everything and will remind you of everything I have told you" (John 14:26).

> "But I will send you the Advocate—the Spirit of truth. He will come to you from the Father and will testify all about me" (John 15:26).

> "But in fact, it is best for you that I go away, because if I don't, the Advocate won't come. If I do go away,

then I will send him to you. And when he comes, he will convict the world of its sin, and of God's righteousness, and of the coming judgment" (John 16:7-8).

"When the Spirit of truth comes, he will guide you into all truth. He will not speak on his own but will tell you what he has heard. He will tell you about the future. He will bring me glory by telling you whatever he receives from me" (John 16:13-14).

The Holy Spirit Is a Presence

The evening was no doubt filled with emotion, but imagine how dumbfounded the disciples must have been when Jesus said, "It is best for you that I go away." Why would he say something like this to the group he had spent the last three years with? Because Jesus knew that when the Holy Spirit came to them, he would be with each one of them always. But that wouldn't happen until Jesus had departed from them.

You see, when Jesus was with his disciples, his presence was localized. He was present with them only when he was with them in person, in his human body. On this last night with his disciples, Jesus knew that he would be crucified and buried, only to rise again three days later and then ascend into heaven (Acts 1:9-11), where he is now seated next to God the Father, praying for us:

> Christ Jesus who died—more than that, who was raised to life—is at the right hand of God and is also interceding for us (Romans 8:34 NIV).

This is why Jesus promised the Holy Spirit. While Jesus is away preparing a place in heaven and praying for all who believe, the Holy Spirit is the presence of Jesus in us. Here's how the apostle Paul explains it. Again, notice how all three persons in the Trinity are involved:

> Because we are his children, God has sent the Spirit
> of his Son into our hearts, prompting us to call out,
> "Abba, Father" (Galatians 4:6).

What Does the Holy Spirit Do for You?

Now that you know who the Holy Spirit is, it's equally important to know what the Holy Spirit does for you. Another way to look at it is this: It's one thing to know *about* the Holy Spirit, and quite another to *know* the Holy Spirit. And the way to do that is to know what he does for you. Here are seven things the Holy Spirit does in the life of every Christian. The first five are initiated by him. The last two are your responsibility.

The Holy Spirit Convicts You

There is a reason why you decided to become a Christian. The Holy Spirit convicted you of your sin and your inability to meet the perfect standard of a holy God (Romans 3:23). Now, to someone who doesn't understand the backstory of salvation, the words *convicted* and *sin* may sound a little harsh, but these are the words Jesus used when he told his disciples the Holy Spirit would "convict the world of its sin, and of God's righteousness, and of the coming judgment" (John 16:8).

We need to thank God that the Holy Spirit does this in our lives, because left on our own, we don't naturally seek God (Psalm 14:2-3; Romans 3:10-12). Consequently, God needs to get our attention, and the way he does that is through the convicting work of the Holy Spirit. You felt this when you said yes to Jesus and decided to accept him as Lord and Savior. You were convicted and convinced that you needed Jesus to forgive you of your sins and to cleanse you of all unrighteousness (1 John 1:9).

The Holy Spirit Regenerates You

Conviction is the first step in the process of becoming a Christian. The next step is regeneration, and it's accomplished by the Holy Spirit. Spiritual regeneration is similar to biological regeneration. It has to do with restoration and new growth. In his letter to Titus, Paul explains what happens when you become a Christian. Watch how the Father, Son, and Holy Spirit work together in this supernatural spiritual process, and how the love of God brings this all about:

> When God our Savior revealed his kindness and love, he saved us, not because of the righteous things we had done, but because of his mercy. He washed away our sins, giving us a new birth and new life through the Holy Spirit. He generously poured out the Spirit upon us through Jesus Christ our Savior. Because of his grace he made us right in his sight and gave us confidence that we will inherit eternal life (Titus 3:4-7).

The Holy Spirit Indwells You

Once the Holy Spirit regenerates you from death to life, he moves into your life. The word for this is *indwelling*. Literally, the Holy

Spirit—promised by Jesus—moves in. This isn't a metaphor. It's real. Your body becomes a dwelling place for the Holy Spirit:

> Don't you realize that your body is the temple of the Holy Spirit, who lives in you and was given to you by God? You do not belong to yourself, for God bought you with a high price. So you must honor God with your body (1 Corinthians 6:19-20).

And it's not just your physical body that the Holy Spirit indwells. He also moves into your heart, soul, and mind.

The Holy Spirit Baptizes You

This one is a little tricky, because when we say "baptism," you are probably thinking about water baptism, which is desirable for a new Christian as an outward demonstration of what has happened on the inside. We'll cover water baptism in chapter 4, but now we want to talk about getting baptized into the collective body of Christ known as the church, which includes all Christians for all time—past, present, and future.

The moment you received Jesus into your life and became a Christian, you were baptized by the Holy Spirit into the body of Christ (1 Corinthians 12:13). In a very real sense, you automatically became a member of the family of God. That means every believer in every part of the world is your spiritual brother or sister.

The Holy Spirit Seals and Assures You

We've cowritten a lot of books and answered thousands of emails from readers asking questions about God, the Bible, and how to live the Christian life. By far the most common question we are asked is this: "How can I know if I am truly saved?" It's a difficult question with an easy answer. You can know you are saved because the Holy Spirit is your guarantee. Here's how the apostle Paul explains it:

> Now it is God who makes both us and you stand firm in Christ. He anointed us, set his seal of ownership on us, and put his Spirit in our hearts as a deposit, guaranteeing what is to come (2 Corinthians 1:21-22 NIV).

The word *seal* had great meaning in biblical times. When something was sealed, it was an official mark showing that a down payment had been made to purchase something. In effect, the seal guaranteed final payment. That's the assurance you have, and it is automatic. Once the Holy Spirit convicts, regenerates, indwells, and baptizes you, he assures you that the plan of salvation authored by God, accomplished by Jesus, and applied by the Holy Spirit is real and irrevocable. It's why Jesus can say,

> "I give them eternal life, and they will never perish. No one can snatch them away from me, for my Father has given them to me, and he is more powerful than anyone else. No one can snatch them from the Father's hand" (John 10:28-29).

The Holy Spirit Fills You

To this point, everything the Holy Spirit does for you is automatic. Just as there is nothing you can do to earn your salvation (Ephesians 2:8-9), there's nothing you can do to trigger the Holy Spirit's work of convicting, regenerating, indwelling, baptizing, and sealing. To put it plainly, there's nothing you can do to become a Christian except to receive by faith what God has already done for you through Jesus and the Holy Spirit. But when it comes to living the Christian life, you need to be proactive. Even though the Holy Spirit lives in you, it's up to you to let him control you.

Remember, you are a temple for the Holy Spirit. The word *temple* is a bit formal, so think of your body/heart/soul/mind as a house. The Holy Spirit already lives in your house, but he doesn't necessarily have the freedom to live in every part of your house because (like every Christian) you tend to close off certain rooms to the Holy Spirit because of self-conceit, neglect, or sin.

That's why Paul uses the declarative verb when he says, "Be filled with the Holy Spirit" (Ephesians 5:18). It's up to you to let him fill you so he can control your thoughts and actions, your words and intentions. And by the way, it's a daily process and it's sometimes difficult because it involves confessing your sins, asking forgiveness of God and others, and taking the initiative to mend broken relationships.

As D.L. Moody once observed, "We are leaky vessels, and we have to keep right under the fountain all the time to keep full of Christ."[2] That's what it means to be filled with the Holy Spirit. It doesn't make you a Christian, but being filled with the Holy Spirit enables you to live your Christian life the way God wants you to.

The Holy Spirit Guides You

Besides being filled with the Holy Spirit, the other positive action you take on is to invite the Holy Spirit to guide you day by day and step by step. When the Holy Spirit is your guide, you resist the urge to give in to "what your sinful nature craves" (Galatians 5:16). Instead, your life produces what the Bible calls the "fruit of the Spirit." Paul lists these in three clusters of character qualities (Galatians 5:22-23):

- *Love, Joy, Peace*—These characterize your relationship with God.
- *Patience, Kindness, Goodness*—These virtues guide your relationships with others.
- *Faithfulness, Gentleness, Self-Control*—These focus on your inner life.

AN ESSENTIAL FOR NEW CHRISTIANS

Jesus used the vine and branches as an illustration of the way his followers are to live (John 15:5-8). Jesus is the vine, and we are the branches, and apart from him we can't produce spiritual fruit. Jesus further explained that the evidence of a fruit-bearing life is the love we have for others, especially those who are also branches of the true vine. Because Jesus loves us so much, he asks—no, he *commands*—that we love each other in the same way he loves us (John 15:12). It's not an easy assignment, so Jesus made this amazing offer to all who follow him:

> "You didn't choose me. I chose you. I appointed you to go and produce lasting fruit, so that the Father will give you whatever you ask for, using my name. This is my command: Love each other" (John 15:16-17).

Q&A
What's the Difference Between God, Jesus, and the Holy Spirit?

This is a question about the Trinity, a word that is actually never mentioned in the Bible, and yet is central to everything the Bible teaches. It's the idea that there is one God, but he is one God in three persons: Father, Son, and Holy Spirit.

How can God be three persons? First of all, you don't have three gods. There is one God, and apart from him there is no other (Isaiah 45:5). But there is a "three-in-oneness" to God that is taught in Scripture. In other words, there is only one God, but within that unity are three eternal and coequal persons, all sharing the same essence and substance, but each having a distinct existence. Consequently, there is both unity and diversity in God.

This is not illogical, but it is a dense idea. It takes serious thought to deal with it, but it's an idea worth thinking about, because each person is engaged in your life:

- God the Father had it in his heart to provide a way for you to be forgiven of your sins, so he *authored* the plan of salvation.
- Jesus the Son, while fully God, submitted to the Father's plan. As the sacrifice for our sins, Jesus *accomplished* the plan of salvation.
- The Holy Spirit, just as much God as the other two persons, is at work in your life because you've chosen

to follow God. The Holy Spirit *applies* the plan of salvation.

When you think about everything the three-in-one God has done for you and how much he loves you, your best response can only be one of awe and wonder and gratitude. So go ahead, thank God for the great things he has done and continues to do in your life.

Part Two

Enjoy the Adventure of Loving God

Chapter 4

Love the Church

To many people, especially new believers, the word *church* can be confusing. In twenty-first century Christian parlance, we think of church as a building where religious people hold their meetings. We meet *at* church. We give money *to* the church. We fall asleep *in* church. These expressions categorize church as a place. But that is not how the New Testament uses the term. When the Bible refers to "the church," it is describing all Christians, or a specific group of Christians, who share the common belief that Jesus Christ is their Lord and Savior. So, when you read what Jesus said to Peter in Matthew 16:18, you know that Jesus is referring to the fact that Peter will be instrumental in bringing people to Christ as the gospel spreads in the Mediterranean region.

> "Now I say to you that you are Peter (which means 'rock'), and upon this rock I will build my **church**, and all the powers of hell will not conquer it" (emphasis added).

Similarly, when you read Acts 15:31, be thinking about people who are bonded together by a common love of Christ, not buildings.

There was great joy throughout the **church** that day
as they read this encouraging message (emphasis
added).

An "As I Have Loved You" Kind of Love

As you will read in chapter 8, God wants us to care for all people
("love your neighbor"), so of course this would mean other Christians.
But the New Testament reveals that Christians are supposed to have a
deeper love and commitment to each other. Jesus explained this to the
disciples in the upper room on the night before he was crucified. This
is when Jesus was giving them instructions for how to live after he was
no longer present on earth:

> "Now I am giving you a new commandment: Love
> each other. Just as I have loved you, you should love
> each other" (John 13:34).

Jesus told his disciples that he wanted them to "love each other."
But notice two things:

First, Jesus said this was a *new* commandment. It had to mean
something different than the "love your neighbor" commandment
given by God (through Moses) to the Jews about 1,500 years earlier.

Second, Jesus qualified the *degree* of love he wanted the disciples
to have for each other: He instructed them to love each other "just as I
have loved you." In about 24 hours those disciples were going to witness Christ's crucifixion. They would see that Jesus loved them enough
to die for them. That was a display of the type of self-sacrificial love
Jesus had for his disciples. That is the degree of love he wanted them to
have for each other.

And that same degree of love—self-sacrificial love—is what Christ wants his followers in the twenty-first century to display for each other. God probably won't ask you to die on a cross for another Christian, but he certainly expects you to be willing to make some personal sacrifice (of your time, your talent, or your resources) for other Christians, just as he wants them to be available to minister to you as your needs require.

A Family and a Body

God reinforces this principal of the unity among believers with two analogies in the Bible, both illustrating God's design for cohesiveness among Christians.

Christians Are a Family

The New Testament uses terms that characterize a spiritual family relationship. God is our heavenly father, and we are his children.

> See how very much our Father loves us, for he calls us his children, and that is what we are! But the people who belong to this world don't recognize that we are God's children because they don't know him (1 John 3:1).

By our salvation through Christ, all believers have been elevated to the status of God's adopted children. That makes us brothers and sisters in Christ. Most families have siblings that squabble. The Christian family is no different, so you will frequently read in the New Testament that God wants his family to live in harmony. Notice how the apostle Paul talked to the group of Christians in the city of Corinth:

> I appeal to you, dear brothers and sisters, by the
> authority of our Lord Jesus Christ, to live in har-
> mony with each other. Let there be no divisions
> in the church. Rather, be of one mind, united in
> thought and purpose (1 Corinthians 1:10).

Christians Are One Body

For local churches, the Bible uses the analogy of a human body to describe how the Christians in that group should function together. Each Christian in a local church comes from a different background, with different life experiences and different journeys getting to Christ. Despite these differences, the most important part of each of their lives is Christ. The Bible says that these Christians are in one body because they are in Christ.

> The human body has many parts, but the many parts
> make up one whole body. So it is with the body
> of Christ. Some of us are Jews, some are Gentiles,
> some are slaves, and some are free. But we have all
> been baptized into one body by one Spirit, and we
> all share the same Spirit (1 Corinthians 12:12-13).

This "one body" analogy is also used by the apostle Paul when he writes about the spiritual gifts used in the church. The Holy Spirit has supernaturally equipped you with a spiritual gift that is to be specifi-cally used for the benefit of your church family. All of you, working together, are like a body that functions with many different parts.

> Yes, the body has many different parts, not just one
> part. If the foot says, "I am not a part of the body

because I am not a hand," that does not make it any less a part of the body. And if the ear says, "I am not part of the body because I am not an eye," would that make it any less a part of the body? If the whole body were an eye, how would you hear? Or if your whole body were an ear, how would you smell anything? But our bodies have many parts, and God has put each part just where he wants it (1 Corinthians 12:14-18).

Baptism and Communion

In Old Testament times, the Jews had several feasts and celebrations, all designed to help them focus on God. The same is true now (in New Testament times) for Christians. These feasts and celebrations are often referred to as *ordinances* of the church. In keeping with God's principle of unity, harmony, and shared experiences of the members of the local church, these ordinances are most often celebrated when the church family meets together:

Baptism

This is an event that celebrates a person's decision to accept Christ as Savior and commit to follow him. During the first century, it was usually performed in a river or lake with the new believer being dunked under the water (symbolizing the death of the old nature) and being brought back up out of the water (symbolizing the new life, just as when Jesus was resurrected from the dead).

Two thousand years later, it can still be done in a lake, but many churches have a specially designed dunking tank (called the *baptistry*). These baptisms are done publicly because it is a time of celebration for the entire church (the dunkee, the dunker, and the audience of church members). This has nothing to do with salvation per se; it is simply a believer's public announcement of being a follower of Christ. One baptism per person is all that is necessary. Christians are big on baptism because Jesus said we should do it.

> "Therefore, go and make disciples of all the nations, baptizing them in the name of the Father and the Son and the Holy Spirit" (Matthew 28:19).

Communion

As we discussed in chapter 3, the night before he was crucified, Jesus had dinner with his disciples ("the Last Supper"), and he gave them a spoiler alert about his impending crucifixion. He used a piece of bread and a sip of wine to represent what would happen to him on the cross:

> On the night when he was betrayed, the Lord Jesus took some bread and gave thanks to God for it. Then he broke it in pieces and said, "This is my body, which is given for you. Do this in remembrance of me." In the same way, he took the cup of wine after supper, saying, "This cup is the new covenant between God and his people—an agreement confirmed with my blood. Do this in remembrance of me as often as you drink it" (1 Corinthians 11: 23-25).

Notice the "do this in remembrance of me" statements. Many churches take this instruction very seriously, celebrating communion every Sunday or one Sunday a month. It is considered a sacred time for Christians as they focus their thoughts on the suffering of Christ on the cross for their sins. Some churches pass trays of bread and a glass of wine (one sip per person) down the aisles. Other churches have trays with itty bitty crackers and thimble-sized cups of grape juice. Most churches emphasize that participation in communion is reserved for people who have accepted Christ as their Savior.

AN ESSENTIAL FOR NEW CHRISTIANS

Think about what is implied by the discussion above. God wants you in a church because that's where Christians love one another sacrificially. Church is a family with brothers and sisters in Christ. It is one body. It is Christians celebrating baptisms and communion. God wants you to be a part of all this. He doesn't want you on the sidelines. He wants you in the mix with other Christians. God is going to use them to work in you, and he is going to use you to work in them and love them.

Q&A
WHAT CHURCH DOES GOD WANT ME TO ATTEND?

Let's start by asking: What is God's purpose for your life? Here is a good verse to get you started:

> Trust in the LORD with all your heart;
>   do not depend on your own understanding.

> Seek his will in all you do,
>> and he will show you which path to take.
>>> (Proverbs 3:5-6)

God wants an intimate relationship with you. He wants you to know him so well that you can put your complete trust in him and know his will for your life. So, as a new Christian, you might want to find a church that will help you get to know God better and fall deeper in love with Jesus. Look for a church that will help you grow and mature as a Christian through:

- sermons that are firmly rooted in the Bible
- times of worship where you focus on God's character
- times of prayer during which you can praise God but also speak openly with him about your concerns
- discipleship groups where you can be mentored by Christians who have a long track record of walking with the Lord
- opportunities for you to serve others in your church and in your community

Look for a church that will accept you as you currently are, but that cares enough to help you receive the conviction of the Holy Spirit in manageable doses to become more like Christ. Do not hesitate to ask if there is someone who would be suitable to help you learn more about what it means to be a Christ-follower. The best church for you will be the one that helps you know Christ better and helps you understand the love and grace he has for you.

Chapter 5

Experience God's Word

You are nearly halfway through this book, and it's time we talked about another book—the Bible. Actually, we have been quoting the Bible in every chapter because the Bible tells us what we need to know about God, Jesus, the Holy Spirit, the church, how to be saved, how to live as a Christian, and where we will spend eternity. But we haven't yet talked about the Bible itself and why it's vital to your life as a new Christian to get to know this book better.

The Bible is unlike any other book ever written. And yet, many people who have a Bible rarely read it. There are several reasons for this reluctance. For starters, it's a long book, with more than 750,000 words (although not as long as the Harry Potter series, which has more than a million words). Because it's so big and complex and sometimes hard to understand, the Bible can be intimidating. In addition, the Bible is actually a collection of 66 individual books—39 in the Old Testament and 27 in the New Testament. And the Bible uses almost every literary style: historical narrative, letters, poetry, musical lyrics, prophecy, and biographies.

Because of the Bible's length and complexity, we understand why many people struggle to read it. And yet we believe there is an even bigger reason the Bible is underread and undervalued by so many people, including many Christians. They don't understand and fully appreciate that the Bible is God's personal message to them, revealing his heart, his will, his love, and his purpose for them.

May we suggest that you look at the Bible not as a book to be read but a true story to be experienced. Yes, the Bible has been read by billions of people and continues to be the bestselling book in the world year after year, but what matters most is that the Bible was written for you by God himself.

Imagine that God sent you a text, an email, or a letter. You would drop everything and read it immediately. Well, think of the Bible in the same way. It's God's personal message to you, sent to you so that you can flourish in this world and be prepared for the world to come.

Where Do You Start?

As with any book, the best place to start the Bible is at the beginning, which in the Bible is the Book of Genesis (the word *genesis* means "beginning"). But before you start at the beginning, you have to know something else about the Bible. It's all about Jesus. The person of Jesus and everything he did is the heart and soul of Scripture. Because God's love for the world and for you is expressed in Jesus, everything in the Bible either looks forward to or focuses on Jesus.

To show you how this works, we're going to divide the Bible into six parts or acts. Notice how each of these shows how God creates, relates, and anticipates the world through Jesus.

Act 1: Creation

Out of his great love and awesome power, God created the universe so we, his human creation, could live in a magnificent world. Where is Jesus in the beginning? Writing in the first century to the church in Colossae, the apostle Paul explained the eternal nature of Jesus and his role in creation. Notice how even today, Jesus holds the world together:

> Christ is the visible image of the invisible God.
>> He existed before anything was created and is supreme over all creation,
> for through him God created everything
>> in the heavenly realms and on earth.
> He made the things we can see
>> and the things we can't see—
> such as thrones, kingdoms, rulers, and authorities in the unseen world.
>> Everything was created through him and for him.
> He existed before anything else,
>> and he holds all creation together.
>
> (Colossians 1:15-17)

Act 2: The Fall

The greatest tragedy in human history came soon after the beginning. The human race fell from a place of perfect beauty and harmony with God to a condition of brokenness and separation from God, all because those made in his image—you and me—decided we didn't need God. Because of the fall, the human race remains separated from a holy God, and there's nothing we can do on our own to make things right with God.

But God didn't leave us without hope. Out of his great love for us, God immediately put a beautiful plan into action, centered in Jesus. The foreshadowing of the coming of Jesus to earth is right there in

Genesis. Speaking to Satan, the great tempter who presented humanity with the opportunity to rebel against its Creator, God said:

> "I will cause hostility between you and the woman,
>> and between your offspring and her offspring.
> He will strike your head,
>> and you will strike his heel."
>>>> (Genesis 3:15)

These prophetic words, spoken by God about his Son, guarantee that Jesus will defeat Satan, sin, and death forever.

Act 3: Israel

As part of God's plan to send Jesus to earth as the perfect and permanent sacrifice for sin, God selected a certain group of people to be his chosen nation. Through this one extended family would come the Messiah, the Savior for not just the nation of Israel, but for all who believe in him. The prophet Isaiah, writing 700 years before the birth of Jesus in Bethlehem, said this about the Savior promised by God in Genesis:

> "All right then, the Lord himself will give you the sign. Look! The virgin will conceive a child! She will give birth to a son and will call him Immanuel (which means 'God is with us')" (Isaiah 7:14).

Act 4: Jesus

The name *Immanuel* means "God is with us," and that's exactly who Jesus was and is and always will be. In Jesus, God is literally with us in the flesh. Furthermore, the name *Jesus* means "Savior," because Jesus came to save us from our sins (Matthew 1:21). Jesus saves us by his life and death, and he gives us eternal life by his resurrection. As Jesus explained to Nicodemus,

> "God sent his Son into the world not to judge the world, but to save the world through him" (John 3:17).

Act 5: The Church

Ever since Jesus left the earth to join his Father in heaven, the Holy Spirit has empowered Christians to introduce others to Jesus and join him in his mission to bring hope and healing to our broken world. These are the last words of Jesus, spoken to his disciples who would soon change the world with their bold witness to the life-changing power of Jesus:

> "You will receive power when the Holy Spirit comes upon you. And you will be my witnesses, telling people about me everywhere—in Jerusalem, throughout Judea, in Samaria, and to the ends of the earth" (Acts 1:8).

Act 6: New Creation

On the day Jesus ascended into heaven, two angels told his followers that Jesus "will return from heaven in the same way you saw him go" (Acts 1:11). This is a reality for every Christian: Jesus will return to rescue all who have believed in him and will take them to his eternal home, where there will be no more sadness, crying, pain, or death (Revelation 21:4). And if you die before Jesus returns, you will immediately be in the presence of the one who loves you, died for you, and was raised from the dead so that you could live eternally with him.

> Just as everyone dies because we all belong to Adam, everyone who belongs to Christ will be given new life. But there is an order to this resurrection: Christ was raised as the first of the harvest; then all who belong to Christ will be raised when he comes back (1 Corinthians 15:22-23).

As you read the Bible, these six acts will help you place whatever you are reading into the context of God's story. It's a story that began "before the beginning" and will continue into an eternal future God designed for you to enjoy in the presence of the Father, Son, and Holy Spirit.

Read the Bible with These "I's"

Knowing that Jesus is at the center of the Bible will change the way you read the Bible. But that's not the end of it. As you read and study the Scriptures, the very words will come alive to you because of three supernatural realities. We call these the three "I's" of the Bible: *Inspiration, Interaction,* and *Imagination.*

Inspiration: This Book Is Alive

A good friend of ours places the following sentence at the end of the signature in his emails: *This Book Is Alive!* This line comes from the Bible:

> The word of God is alive and powerful. It is sharper than the sharpest two-edged sword, cutting between soul and spirit, between joint and marrow. It exposes our innermost thoughts and desires (Hebrews 4:12).

The reason the Bible can say this about itself is that this is literally true. The Bible is alive because God wrote it by breathing into the 40 different authors who wrote the 66 books of the Bible. This process is called "inspiration," and it's the reason the Bible is completely true and trustworthy.

> All Scripture is inspired by God and is useful to teach us what is true and to make us realize what is wrong in our lives. It corrects us when we are wrong and teaches us to do what is right (2 Timothy 3:16).

God's breath gives life. In the same way that God breathed into Adam and gave him life (Genesis 2:7), in the same way God breathed the Holy Spirit into your life, God gave life to his word when he breathed into the writers of all 66 books in the Bible. Through the Holy Spirit, God guided these human authors so that their words became the word of God (2 Peter 1:20-21).

Nearly 2,000 years after the last book of the Bible was written, we have the incredible privilege to read those words guided by the same Holy Spirit who inspired—breathed in—the Scriptures in the first place. This should fill us with awe and wonder. The same Holy Spirit who breathed into the Bible writers breathes out God's word directly into our minds and hearts so we can comprehend what is true about God, the world, and ourselves.

Interaction: You Know the Author

Isn't it amazing how all three persons in the Trinity are involved in giving you the Bible? God wrote the Bible through the Holy Spirit and it's all about Jesus. That's why our friend, Pastor Mark Clark, is fond of saying, "The word is how we experience the Word." Every time you open your Bible to read or you listen to someone read the Bible to you, you are literally interacting *in real time* with God in three persons. This means that when you read the Bible, you are experiencing something intimate, loving, and supernatural:

> Because we are his children, God has sent the Spirit
> of his Son into our hearts, prompting us to call out,
> "Abba, Father" (Galatians 4:6).

If the Bible seems difficult to you, ask the Holy Spirit to help you understand. Jesus assures us that the Holy Spirit will guide us into all truth (John 16:13). But it won't happen in a single day or a week or even a year. Knowing Jesus as he is revealed in the Bible and taught to you by the inner working of the Holy Spirit will take time, but what a time it will be as "the Lord—who is the Spirit—will make [you] more and more like him as [you] are changed into his glorious image" (2 Corinthians 3:18).

Imagination: Read with the Eyes of Your Heart

As you read and study the Bible, resist the urge to treat it like a textbook, full of information that you need to understand with your mind. For sure, the Bible will challenge your mind, but your ability to read, understand, and apply the Bible to your life will come from your heart. Here's how Paul explains this process:

> I pray that the eyes of your heart may be enlightened
> in order that you may know the hope to which he
> has called you, the riches of his glorious inheritance
> in his holy people, and his incomparably great power

for us who believe. That power is the same as the mighty strength he exerted when he raised Christ from the dead and seated him at his right hand in the heavenly realms, far above all rule and authority, power and dominion, and every name that is invoked, not only in the present age but also in the one to come (Ephesians 1:18-21 NIV).

This glorious passage should ignite your imagination. It paints a picture of the death, resurrection, and ascension of Jesus, who is now seated at the right hand of the Father, ruling the world we live in. Use your imagination to *experience* what the Bible is saying. For the psalmist, the Bible was so wonderful he could literally taste it:

> How sweet your words taste to me;
>   they are sweeter than honey.
>   (Psalm 119:103)

May you experience the Bible and everything it says about Jesus not just with your physical eyes but with the eyes of your heart.

AN ESSENTIAL FOR NEW CHRISTIANS

Spend quality time with God by studying what he has said in his Word. The Bible is not a collection of "dead letters," but is the living message of our loving God. In return, when you read, experience, and obey the Bible, you are showing God that you love him. Jesus made this clear when he said,

"If you love me, obey my commands" (John 14:15). The apostle John, who recorded those words of Jesus, made it clear that one of those commands is to love each other:

> Love means doing what God has commanded us, and he has commanded us to love one another, just as you heard from the beginning (2 John 6).

Q&A
WHAT'S THE BEST WAY TO READ AND STUDY THE BIBLE?

The words *study* and *Bible* often go together, but studying should never be a substitute for reading. As you read the Bible, imagine that the author is in the room with you giving you insights and encouragement—because that is exactly what is happening when you encounter God's Word. As you read, God will speak to you in the quietness of your Bible study time. And the Holy Spirit will help you understand what you are reading (1 Corinthians 2:10-12).

Practical Tips for Reading and Understanding the Bible

First of all, find a Bible version that you enjoy reading. There are many fine Bible translations that will make the Bible come alive for you. Our top three favorites are the New Living Translation (NLT), the New International Version (NIV), and the English Standard Version (ESV). When you find a Bible version you like, follow these five tips for getting the most out of your Bible reading:

- *Read it all.* Read a book of the Bible in its entirety—in one sitting, or over several days or weeks if the book is longer—so you can better grasp the author's intent.
- *Read it slowly and prayerfully.* Don't read for information but for transformation.
- *Read it with others.* When you're in a group, you will learn from others as they ask questions about what they have read.
- *Read a study Bible or commentary.* These tools will help you better understand the Bible, especially when it comes to context, genre, and historical background.
- *Read it chronologically.* The Bible generally follows a chronological order, and there are specialty Bibles that will help you understand the historical flow.

Chapter 6

Talk to God

Prayer is your opportunity to have a two-way conversation with the Almighty God, the Creator of the universe, the Savior of your soul. Some newbie Christians make the rookie mistake of thinking that their prayer time will be put to better use if they use the opportunity to deliver a monologue.

Get in the Habit of Prayer

For many people, praying doesn't come naturally. It is a bit intimidating (after all, it is God you are talking to). You don't know what to say. And if God is omniscient and always knows everything, doesn't he already know what you are going to say? Is praying to God the ultimate redundancy?

Regardless of any hesitancy you may have about prayer, this is very clear in Scripture: God wants you to pray!

> Devote yourselves to prayer with an alert mind and a thankful heart (Colossians 4:2).

> Always be joyful. Never stop praying. Be thankful in all circumstances, for this is God's will for you who belong to Christ Jesus (1 Thessalonians 5:16-18).

One day Jesus told his disciples a story to show that they should always pray and never give up (Luke 18:1).

Maybe you wonder what you should be praying about. God antici-pated that reaction, so he loaded the Bible with recommendations for your prayer list.

Talk to God About What Worries You

Don't worry about anything; instead, pray about everything. Tell God what you need, and thank him for all he has done. Then you will experience God's peace, which exceeds anything we can understand. His peace will guard your hearts and minds as you live in Christ Jesus (Philippians 4:6-7).

Pray for Other Christians Who Are Enduring Tough Times

Pray in the Spirit at all times and on every occasion. Stay alert and be persistent in your prayers for all be-lievers everywhere (Ephesians 6:18).

Confess Your Sins Through Prayer

If we confess our sins to him, he is faithful and just to forgive us our sins and to cleanse us from all wick-edness (1 John 1:9).

When you make prayer a habit, praising God for his love and thanking him for his provisions for you, you will experience the ben-efits of prayer:

- He has promised that he will never leave or abandon us (Hebrews 13:5).
- He equips us to live a godly life (2 Peter 1:3).
- He is eager to forgive our sins (1 John 1:9).
- He gives us courage when we need it (Joshua 1:9).
- He comforts us in our time of trouble (2 Corinthians 1:3-4).
- He can help us be strong in times of temptation (Hebrews 2:17-18).

The list is endless. God is certainly worthy of such prayers and praises. But he is not dependent upon them. The reason we are instructed to praise God in our prayers is that such prayers remind us of his character. The more we focus on God, the more our prayers become God-centered (aligned with his desires) and less self-centered.

Praying Within God's Will

As you get to know God better, you will trust him more. At some point you will trust that God knows what is best. Even though you may want something else, you will trust God's love and decision more than you trust your own instincts. Bottom line: You will want what he wants for you, even though it might not be your choice.

Jesus gave the best example of aligning our prayers with God's desires. On the night before he was crucified, Jesus was having an intense (he was sweating drops of blood) prayer session with God the Father. Jesus knew that the next day he would be crucified. While he was willing to go down that path, he would have preferred a change of plans. Read carefully how Jesus makes the request for his preference ultimately conditioned upon the will of his Father:

> "Father, if you are willing, please take this cup of suffering away from me. Yet I want your will to be done, not mine" (Luke 22:42).

That's the attitude we should have every time we pray. There is nothing wrong with telling God what result we would like, but in the event that our desired result is not God's desired result, we should willingly welcome what he wants for us. This concept is often referred to as "praying in accordance with God's will." It means that when we pray about a certain issue, we are willing to accept whatever outcome God allows as his perfect and acceptable answer to our prayers. This is the approach to prayer for a spiritually mature Christian.

When you read Bible passages about prayer, keep in mind that most passages already assume that you will be praying in accordance with God's will. Otherwise, the Bible verses could be misunderstood. A classic example was written by King David:

> Take delight in the LORD,
> > and he will give you your heart's desires.
> > > (Psalm 37:4)

This verse does not mean that Jesus will give you whatever you want if you wish for it with all your heart. The verse is premised on the concept that God becomes the focus of our life; we find our joy in him, not in our possessions or circumstances. When our prayer life is God-centered (when we are delighting in him), then our prayers are aligned with what he wants for us. Through the Holy Spirit, we will desire what God wants us to desire. Within that relationship, we desire to know more about God and love him more deeply. God is eager to answer a prayer for those desires.

Similarly, it is easy to get tripped up by John 16:24, a statement by Jesus that often gets misquoted as "Ask and you shall receive." (Sounds like something a genie would say, right?) Actually, the verse reads like this:

> "Ask, using my name, and you will receive, and you
> will have abundant joy."

Did you notice the clue that implies that this is a prayer made according to God's will? Jesus was specifically talking about prayers made "using his name"—in other words, prayers that were made to God seeking to be aligned with his will. If you say a prayer asking to get rich (even if you say, "I pray *in the name of Jesus* for one million dollars") it is doubtful that you will receive what you asked for. The Bible promises that God "will supply all your needs" (Philippians 4:19), but that is not an open-ended promise to grant greedy, self-centered prayers.

What Should You Do When You Pray?

Many people who say yes to Jesus have never prayed previously. The "I accept you as my Savior" prayer was the first prayer they ever uttered. Many of them didn't grow up in a family culture that included prayers, and they might not have logged many (if any) hours in church.

If this is you, it is understandable that you might be terrified about praying in public or even privately to God. Relax.

When there is prayer time in a church service, just take a cue from the people around you. Most likely, the only person talking out loud will be standing on the platform. Just stay still. Stand up when people stand up. Sit down when people sit down. If somebody announces that everybody should "keep your heads bowed and your eyes closed," you can comply. It is doubtful that someone will try to steal your wallet when you aren't looking.

It is even easier when you are praying privately with God. You can sit or stand or kneel or lie on the bed. You can fold your hands or stick them in your pockets. Yes, you are talking to the Creator of the universe, so you should be respectful. But God loves you and is eager to spend time in prayer with you because you are his new child whose salvation was purchased by the blood of Jesus. Just talk to God. No Shakespearean accent required. God doesn't really care about your posture, your hand gestures, or the sophistication of your vocabulary. But he is interested in your thoughts and your attitudes.

But don't forget to spend time listening. Don't be quick to say, "That's all I got, Lord. Over and out." (FYI, a traditional close to your prayer might be something like, "in Jesus' name I pray, amen.") As your prayer comes to an end, spend some quiet time with God. Don't expect to hear angel voices, but you might want to allow the Holy Spirit some time to speak to you through your thoughts. Meditate on a few Bible verses that describe God's character. God knows your thoughts, and he wants you to know his thoughts about you.

An Essential for New Christians

On the night Jesus was betrayed, he met with his disciples in what is commonly called the Last Supper. One of the highlights of this dramatic evening is that Jesus prayed for his disciples and for everyone who would believe in him. At the core of his prayer was his desire that all of us who believe in him would be brought into complete unity, which would show the world that God loves us, just as he loves his Son.

> "May they experience such perfect unity that
> the world will know that you sent me and
> that you love them as much as you love me"
> (John 17:23).

But his prayer for us didn't stop there. Because he loves us so much, Jesus continues to pray for us from his place at the right hand of the Father (Romans 8:34). Likewise, he wants you to be in constant conversation with him. Prayer is your direct line of communication with the Almighty God. Use it often.

Q&A
WHAT IF GOD DOESN'T ANSWER MY PRAYER?

You aren't alone in thinking this. It is a common question from people who are on the spiritual learning curve. It seems simple, doesn't it? You are expecting that God has a yes or a no answer to your prayer, and God hasn't given a clear indication either way. But there is a third alternative. Have you considered that God may have given you an answer: not yet.

God continues to stretch the faith of his children. We are usually anxious and want answers right away. God, on the other hand, wants us to learn to wait, to be patient, and to trust in him that he has everything under control. It is part of the sanctification process of spiritual growth.

Remember that God is omniscient (knows everything that is past, present, and future), and he is sovereign (controls everything from the past, in the present, and in the future). At the very moment that you are praying, he might have the wheels in motion to bring about a result for the very thing you are praying about. But his timetable may be far different from yours. So, keep praying in accordance with his will. In the meanwhile, be comforted by this verse:

> We know that God causes everything to work together for the good of those who love God and are called according to his purpose for them (Romans 8:28).

God has not forgotten you. He is causing all of the details to work together for your benefit according to what he knows is best for you.

Chapter 7

Decide to Follow Jesus for the Rest of Your Life

We live in amazing times. Never before in the 2,000-year history of the church have so many people been exposed to the gospel through preaching, the Bible, and the story of Jesus, both in person and through media that is available instantly all over the world. When the first followers of Jesus started telling others about the good news of salvation made possible by the life, death, and resurrection of Jesus, they took the message to the known world on foot. Today, that same message can go out to billions of people instantaneously through our phones and other digital technology. The result is that more people than ever before are coming to faith in Jesus Christ.

You may have first heard the gospel through some kind of media. But it's likely that you responded when someone shared the good news of Jesus with you. It may have been a friend, a pastor in a church, or a speaker at a live event. But it was *someone* who cared enough about you to share the good news with you. And they did it in the same spirit as the apostle Paul, who said,

> I am not ashamed of this Good News about Christ.
> It is the power of God at work, saving everyone

who believes—the Jew first and also the Gentile (Romans 1:16).

Paul's statement shows how the gospel is:

- *Bold*—We don't need to be ashamed of it.
- *Powerful*—The power of God makes it possible.
- *Saving*—This is the only power that can truly change lives.
- *For everyone*—Anyone can receive the saving life of Jesus.

This is the good news you have received and accepted by faith. And now that you are a Christian, you have a decision to make. Do you want to remain the way you are, or do you want to grow in your faith as a true follower of Jesus Christ, helping others to discover his saving life just as you have?

Steps to Growing as a Christian

So far in this book, we have outlined the steps you need to take in order to grow as a Christian. And make no mistake about it, you need to grow! When you were "born again," you were like a baby needing nourishment and constant care. But just as you can't remain a baby in the physical sense, you can't stay a baby in the spiritual sense. You need to grow up.

The spiritual growth process begins by getting to know the three-person God: Father, Son, and Holy Spirit. You can't grow alone; you need community, which is why it's so important to get involved with a local church, where you hear solid Bible teaching, participate in the ordinances God has designed for his family, and discover your spiritual gifts so you can serve others. You are experiencing the Bible, not as a textbook but as the living word of God written for your benefit. And you are learning to communicate with God in real time through prayer.

All of these steps in your new Christian life are critical for your growth, and they are yours to enjoy and benefit from for the rest of your life. But you're not done. There's something else Jesus wants you to do, and it is without question one of the most important assignments you will ever have. Are you ready? Here's your assignment: *Make disciples.*

The Great Commission

This assignment, known as the Great Commission, comes directly from Jesus. It was one of the last things he told his disciples, and it was so important that you will find it in all four of the Gospels, as well as the Book of Acts. Here is the Great Commission as recorded by Matthew:

> Jesus came and told his disciples, "I have been given all authority in heaven and on earth. Therefore, go and make disciples of all the nations, baptizing them in the name of the Father and the Son and the Holy Spirit. Teach these new disciples to obey all the commands I have given you. And be sure of this: I am with you always, even to the end of the age" (Matthew 28:18-20).

Notice that the only direct command in the Great Commission is to "make disciples." The instructions to *go, baptize,* and *teach* are indirect commands that flow from the primary directive to *make disciples.* Simply put, they are the means by which we make disciples. But before we talk about making disciples, we need to answer two questions: What does it mean to be a disciple? And what is involved in discipleship?

What Is a Disciple?

The word *disciple,* which occurs 269 times in the New Testament, is most commonly used to describe a teacher-student relationship. That was true when the original 12 disciples were called to follow Jesus, and it's true today. As a disciple of Jesus Christ, he is your teacher, and you are his student. You *learn* from Jesus as you *follow* him. But in the process of following and learning from Jesus, there are three requirements:

> Then Jesus said to his disciples, "Whoever wants to be my disciple must deny themselves and take up their cross and follow me" (Matthew 16:24 NIV).

At first glance these three requirements appear to be difficult. But maybe that's the point. Being a disciple of Jesus is serious business.

Deny Yourself

When Jesus calls for his disciples to deny themselves, he's not saying we should think less of ourselves. Rather, he is saying we should think of ourselves less. The human tendency is to look out for number one. We are by nature filled with pride and selfish ambition, but the moment we are transformed into a new creation in Jesus Christ, our nature changes. No longer are we motivated by self-interest. By God's grace and with his help, we begin to think of others more highly than ourselves. As A.W. Tozer writes, "He loves you too well and too much to let you continue to strut and boast and cultivate your egotism and feed your I."[3]

Take Up Your Cross

It's easy to take these four words the wrong way. We get this picture in our minds of Jesus struggling to carry his cross to his execution, and we assume that God wants us to endure the same kind of physical and emotional stress that Jesus did. In other words, look out, because as a Christian you're going to experience a lot of pain and suffering. There's no question that your new life in Jesus does not protect you from *suffering*, but Jesus is more concerned about *submission*.

Crucifixion was a common method of execution in the Roman world. When taken to be crucified, the convicted criminal was forced to carry his own cross as a public symbol that he was submissive to the rule he had rebelled against. In the same way, disciples of Jesus demonstrate their submission to the one true God they have rebelled against by "taking up their cross." Taking up your cross isn't so much about personal hardship as it is about dying to your own will and taking up God's will. Indeed, Jesus set the example for us when he took up his cross in submission to the Father's will. As F.B. Meyer writes,

> Let us be more eager to lose ourselves than to find ourselves; more set on the cross than on the glory; more eager to promote the well-being of others than our own. We do not choose or make our cross; Christ gives each a little bit of his true cross to bear as he pleases.[4]

Follow Me

Leadership is all the rage these days. It's a common belief that if you want to succeed in life, you have to lead. But Jesus calls us to a different way of living. He invites us to *follow* him. In fact, as Rick Langer and Joanne Jung write in their excellent book, *The Call to Follow,* "The general hallmark of the faithful Christian is being a faithful follower."[5]

Following Jesus includes both *abandonment* and *attachment*. As a follower of Jesus, you may have to abandon those things that distract you from him and your desire to grow into spiritual maturity. As you shift your allegiances, you will more naturally attach yourself to Jesus. However, just because you shift your mindset from leadership to followership doesn't mean you will never lead. You will simply lead in a way that draws others to Jesus. This is what *discipleship* is all about.

What Is Discipleship?

Discipleship isn't a program where you get a degree. It's a process and a relationship where you follow Jesus as a lifelong teacher and friend, learning from his life and words, imitating him in all aspects of life. As Dallas Willard said, "You live your life the way Jesus would live your life if he had your life to live."[6]

Here's another way to look at it. When you said yes to Jesus, it was as if you were making a wedding vow, committing yourself to him for the rest of your life (only death will never separate you). But what good is a wedding without a marriage? Imagine saying yes to your wife or husband, and then wandering off to live somewhere else. The wedding would be meaningless.

So it is with your commitment to Jesus. Your yes is only as good as the life you live with him. Discipleship is the heavenly marriage between you and Jesus. And like an earthly marriage, the relationship between you and Jesus is often slow and sometimes messy, but ultimately the most satisfying, enjoyable, and rewarding experience anyone could have in this life.

The life of discipleship involves your entire being: your head, your heart, and your hands:

- *Your head*—You need to become a student of the Bible, which is the word of God centered on the Word of God.
- *Your heart*—You need to build relationships with other believers by getting involved in a local church, where you can use your spiritual gifts.
- *Your hands*—The world is a broken place that needs compassionate people to step into the lives and circumstances of those in need.

How Do You Make Disciples?

Now we're getting to the core of Christ's Great Commission. This is his primary directive, and it's the key to following Jesus for the rest of your life. That's why you need to develop the lifestyle of making disciples.

Now, let's be clear. Only God can make someone into a lifelong follower of Jesus. Spiritual transformation is the work of God, accomplished by Jesus, and applied by the Holy Spirit. But the commitment to spiritual growth is our responsibility. Only it's not something we can do alone. We need help if we truly desire to become a follower of Jesus.

When Jesus called his disciples, he didn't leave them alone. He taught them and they learned from him. He walked with them, ate with them, and went through hard times with them. In short, Jesus did life with his followers. What Jesus did with his disciples is what he wants us to do with others. He wants us to do life with them by teaching, learning, walking, eating, and going through hard times with them so we can all become lifelong followers of Jesus. That's what it means to make disciples.

Where Do You Begin?

As a new Christian, you may wonder if you need a little time before you start teaching others. Well, yes and no. You need a little time for the seed of the gospel to take root in your life. You need a little time to grow. But you don't want to wait too long. Growing as a Christian is a lifelong process based on a relationship with Jesus. It's a way of life, not a program where you earn a degree. Likewise, being a disciple and making disciples is not a program, but a lifelong process based on a relationship with Jesus and other people. And that's a process you can begin immediately.

In his excellent book *The Complete Book of Discipleship,* Bill Hull uses the concept of mentoring as a framework for disciple making. "Mentoring helps others make sense of their lives," he writes, "and spiritual mentoring helps an individual gain awareness of his personhood as he lives under God."[7]

As a follower of Jesus, you need a spiritual mentor, and in time you also need to become a mentor. It's natural to think that your mentor needs to be older than you, while the person you are mentoring should be younger. Age has nothing to do with it. A spiritually mature twenty-something could easily mentor a new Christian in their sixties. The key is to become a lifelong learner, even as you teach others.

This process won't happen on its own. You need to pray that God leads you to the right person or people to mentor you and also leads you to someone for you to mentor. As you are being discipled and you are discipling others, prepare your heart and your mind to engage with the Bible and other resources you will be studying together. Most of all, have a spirit of humility and submission as you deny yourself, take up your cross, and follow Jesus.

AN ESSENTIAL FOR NEW CHRISTIANS

Being a disciple and making disciples depends on having deep spiritual relationships with others. Because of the bond we share in Jesus, who loves us so much, it may be that these brothers and sisters in Christ will become our closest friends. And if we truly love them the way Jesus loves us, we will literally be willing to lay down our lives for them, just as Jesus did for us. That's why Jesus called this "the greatest love" (John 15:13).

As you seriously commit to being a disciple of Jesus, the Holy Spirit's work in you will help you talk with others about your faith in Christ. Having a spiritual mentor will accelerate your knowledge and understanding of God. In the supernatural progression that the Lord has in mind for you, don't be surprised when you find yourself eager and comfortable in bringing others to Christ.

Q&A
WHAT'S THE BEST WAY TO DO DISCIPLESHIP?

There are two ways to engage with others in a discipleship journey: one-on-one and in a group (notice we didn't say "by yourself").

We have participated in both of these frameworks, and both have been effective. However, our experience is that discipleship and disciple making are more effective in a group. Having more personalities involved is both enriching and challenging.

God made us to be in community, and we are more likely to thrive with a group of people who are growing together spiritually than we would with just one other person. Besides, this is the way Jesus taught his disciples. He had his large group of 12 and his inner circle of three.

Bill Hull offers five principles for every group. Whether you are the leader or a member of a group, these are excellent guidelines:

- *Be intentional*—If you're a leader, don't promise more than you can deliver, and if you are a member, don't expect the group to meet all your spiritual needs.
- *Provide structure*—Develop a statement of purpose for the group, one that will help the members develop good habits and reach their goals.
- *Strive for intimacy*—Create an atmosphere that allows people to lower their defenses and be authentic.
- *Insist on outreach*—Don't close the group off to new people. You're a group, not a clique.
- *Commit to reproduce*—If you're a member, your goal should be to someday lead a discipleship group. If you're a leader, look for others who could become leaders.[8]

Part Three

Experience the Joy
of Loving Others

Chapter 8

Love Your Neighbor

The story must be pretty important. There are three versions of it in the New Testament (see Matthew 22, Mark 12, and Luke 10). Jesus is speaking to a large group of Jews. A guy comes out of the crowd, walks up to Jesus, and asks a theological question. If you translate that question into twenty-first century lingo, you roughly get: "What does it take to become a Christian?"

Jesus gives him a two-part answer:

1. "You must love the LORD your God with all your heart, all your soul, all your strength, and all your mind."

That doesn't surprise anybody. The crowd mumbles with approval to that command; there is a lot of head nodding, and the older men are stroking their beards as if to give Jesus tacit agreement. What Jesus said is *not* one of the famous Ten Commandments, but it is a well-embedded command in Jewish law ever since Moses said it 1,600 years earlier. And the command is so broad that it covers at least the first four of the Ten Commandments.

But then Jesus throws in a shocker, almost to say, "Oh yeah, and there's another one, and if you do them both, you've basically got everything covered":

2. "Love your neighbor as yourself."

The heads in the crowd snap back. The nodding stops. The Jews were good with loving God, but there was a lot of bad blood between the Jews and the Samaritans (who lived in the neighboring region of Samaria), Romans (who lived among the Jews), and anyone else who wasn't 100 percent Jewish. For the Jews, "Love your neighbor" was an acceptable rule only if, by definition, your neighbor was a Jew.

Hoping for a loophole that would allow the Jews to retain their present prejudices, the guy asks Jesus a follow-up question: "Who is my neighbor?"

Jesus knows his answer to this loaded question will blow their sandals off, so he tells everybody to sit down, and then he proceeds to tell the parable of the Good Samaritan. (Remember that these people had just been told that the "Love Your Neighbor" command was just as important as the "Love God" command.)

> "There was once a [Jewish] man traveling from Jeru-
> salem to Jericho. On the way he was attacked by rob-
> bers. They took his clothes, beat him up, and went
> off leaving him half-dead. Luckily, a [Jewish] priest
> was on his way down the same road, but when he
> saw him he angled across to the other side. Then
> a [Jewish] Levite religious man showed up; he also
> avoided the injured man.
>
> "A Samaritan [those who were despised by the Jews]
> traveling the road came on him. When he saw the
> man's condition, his heart went out to him. He
> gave him first aid, disinfecting and bandaging his

wounds. Then he lifted him onto his donkey, led him to an inn, and made him comfortable. In the morning he took out two silver coins and gave them to the innkeeper, saying, 'Take good care of him. If it costs any more, put it on my bill—I'll pay you on my way back'" (Luke 10:30-35 MSG).

The crowd squirms nervously. They know what is coming. Jesus asks this penetrating question: "Now which of these three would you say was a neighbor to the man who was attacked by bandits?"

Along with what everybody else was thinking, the guy who started the discussion meekly replies: "The one who showed him mercy."

To which Jesus replies: "Yes, now go and do the same."

Who Is Your Neighbor?

The point of the parable was painfully obvious to everyone who heard it. Your "neighbor" is anyone you come in contact with who needs help, or care, or comfort. Two millenia later, the point of the parable is painfully obvious to all of us who read it. Not only are we supposed to love Jesus (answer part #1), but we are also supposed to *love the way Jesus loved,* meaning that we must willingly extend kindness to everyone we come in contact with (answer part #2).

You, as a new believer, may be startled by this surprising revelation. Maybe you are confused a bit and thinking: *Hey, I was told salvation is free, with no requirement that I do anything except love Jesus. Now you're saying I have to be a servant to everyone I meet? Ahh, this sounds like religious bait and switch.*

You are correct that salvation is free and is determined only by your decision to love and follow Jesus. As Christ-followers, we are free from rules and regulations because our salvation is rooted in grace, not based on "do and don't" behavioral checklists. But claiming Christ as our Savior means we want to emulate his character. And Christ was all about being a servant. As Jesus said about himself:

> "Whoever wants to be a leader among you must be your servant…For even the Son of Man came not to be served but to serve others and to give his life as a ransom for many" (Matthew 20:26, 28).

And he told those who follow him:

> "If any of you wants to be my follower, you must give up your own way, take up your cross daily, and follow me" (Luke 9:23).

The apostle Paul explained that the essence of Christianity is following Christ's model of servanthood instead of insisting on our freedom:

> You have been called to live in freedom, my brothers and sisters. But don't use your freedom to satisfy your sinful nature. Instead, use your freedom to serve one another in love (Galatians 5:13).

Yes, being a *servant* goes against our selfish human nature. But God knows this. That is why he has the Holy Spirit living inside of you. Don't even think of attempting to love your neighbor in your own strength. Do it in God's strength working through you.

> God has not given us a spirit of fear and timidity, but of power, **love**, and self-discipline (2 Timothy 1:7, emphasis added).

How Do You Show Love to Your Neighbor?

Don't wander around looking for someone you will target as your neighbor. Instead, identify yourself as a neighbor. Assume that role. Be neighborly to everyone. Although the "What Would Jesus Do?" technique might sound clichéd, as you encounter people, consider how Jesus would respond to them. Don't worry. You are not expected to perform any healing miracles; Jesus didn't heal everyone. But he was always quick to give attention to the person who was overlooked by the rest of society.

Because he told the parable of the Good Samaritan, that might be a good resource to see what Jesus thinks "loving your neighbor" looks like.

It Shows Mercy

This is the quality of the Good Samaritan that Jesus mentioned, so let's start with that. In the context of serving others, mercy and compassion are roughly synonymous. They convey the sense of emotional empathy that moves you to respond in loving service. In the parable, the priest and the Levite coldheartedly walked around the bloody body on the road. They saw him, but they intentionally passed him up. It was the despised Samaritan who tenderheartedly picked him up.

It Is Impartial

The Jews considered Samaritans to have pagan ancestry and lukewarm devotion to God. The disdain and racial prejudice held by the Jews against the Samaritans was notorious. But it did not matter to the Good Samaritan that the person he helped would never have reciprocated if the circumstances were reversed. As Christians, we need to see others as Jesus sees them without distinction. Remember, God may be asking you to help a "neighbor" who is not as good looking as you, or as good smelling. They may not live in a house as nice as yours, or in a house at all. Their ethnicity doesn't matter; their politics don't matter; their religion doesn't matter. What matters is that they are a soul for whom Christ died. God wants them to receive a kind, loving gesture, and you are the person he has chosen for the task. How can you be sure? Because he put this person in your path.

It Is Proactive

The Samaritan didn't whisper a cavalier "I'll pray for ya" and then scurry by. Nope, he sprang into action. He took practical measures to care for the victim. He didn't give it minimal effort. He went far beyond. He administered first aid at the crime scene. Then he took the victim to a local B&B. He even told the innkeeper that he would stop by again on his return trip to pay any extra expenses. God is excessive with his blessings on each of us. God is never stingy. Loving your neighbor is not a place for minimum effort. Go overboard, like your heavenly Father does for you.

It Will Be Inconvenient

The Good Samaritan was on a trip. He had an itinerary, and there was no time on his schedule for "help save the life of a robbery victim." He set his own priorities aside to help someone he didn't even know. Loving your neighbor is going to take time. Be willing to give it because, in a real sense, you are giving it to God.

It May Be Costly

The Good Samaritan paid for the victim's lodging at the B&B with his own money. And he promised to pay more if his two silver coins weren't enough. God may call you to spend some of your money (which he has blessed you with) as you show love to your neighbor. Don't quibble about whether it is tax-deductible. God loves a cheerful giver (2 Corinthians 9:7).

AN ESSENTIAL FOR NEW CHRISTIANS

As a new Christian, you are beginning to learn about the immeasurable love that God has for you. He is ecstatic about you. How can you reciprocate his extravagant love? Love your neighbor. Don't use the excuse of waiting until you find someone in the gutter who was just mugged. That is not likely to happen on a daily basis. Instead, be on the lookout for someone who needs help, or a word of encouragement, or an act of kindness. That is likely to happen on a daily basis.

We know what you may be thinking. *I have to be like the Good Samaritan every day?* Let's look at it this way: Just be prepared to love your neighbor as often as God has shown his love toward you.

> Dear children, let's not merely say that we love each other; let us show the truth by our actions. Our actions will show that we belong to the truth, so we will be confident when we stand before God (1 John 3:18-19).

Q&A
HOW DO I GET ALONG WITH PEOPLE I DON'T LIKE?

For each of us, there are people who we find annoying…less than tolerable…let's just say they are "irregular." They won't suddenly become a desirable friendship candidate the moment you are saved. But God would like you to start seeing them that way.

All Christians, before they said yes to Jesus, were wallowing in sin, immorality, and rebellion against God, and we looked worse than irregular. Paul described the human condition (prior to salvation) as worthless filth. In that condition, we were all undesirable. In fact, we were all downright repulsive. And it was precisely when we were in that condition that Jesus loved us.

> You must have the same attitude that Christ Jesus had.
> > Though he was God,
> he did not think of equality with God
> > as something to cling to.
> Instead, he gave up his divine privileges;
> > he took the humble position of a slave
> > and was born as a human being.
> When he appeared in human form,
> > he humbled himself in obedience to God
> > and died a criminal's death on a cross.
> > > (Philippians 2:5-8)

God loved us so much that he allowed his Son to be crucified for us. In gratitude for the magnanimous display of love, forgiveness, mercy, and grace he has extended to us, we should be able to suck it up enough to show kindness to people we don't like. Is that too much for Jesus to ask of us? So, try it. You might actually like it.

> Since God chose you to be the holy people he loves, you must clothe yourselves with tenderhearted mercy, kindness, humility, gentleness, and patience. Make allowance for each other's faults, and forgive anyone who offends you. Remember, the Lord forgave you, so you must forgive others. Above all, clothe yourselves with love, which binds us all together in perfect harmony (Colossians 3:12-14).

Chapter 9

Show Compassion

If there's one word that best describes the attitude and actions of the Good Samaritan, it's compassion. It's also the word that best summarizes how you are to "love your neighbor." The word *compassion* simply means "to suffer with" someone else. Usually, we reserve our compassionate spirit for a relative or a close friend who's going through a difficult time. But what about the people we don't know? How can we express compassion to people who are suffering, no matter who they are or where they live? That's what we want to talk about in this chapter.

Jesus Is Our Example

The supreme model for compassion is Jesus. His compassion for people was tangible and profound. Out of his compassion, Jesus healed the sick (Matthew 14:14) and provided food for people who were hungry (Matthew 14:15-21). At a time when women were considered second-class citizens, he showed extraordinary compassion. Here are three stories from the Bible that prove our point:

First, a woman was caught in adultery, and the religious leaders brought her to Jesus with the intention of humiliating and possibly killing her. They referenced the Law of Moses, which commanded them to stone such women (John 8:1-11). Jesus challenged those who had "never sinned [to] throw the first stone." One by one the accusers walked away, leaving Jesus with the woman. When there was no one left to accuse her, Jesus said, "Neither do I. Go and sin no more."

Second, Jesus showed compassion to the woman at the well (John 4:1-30). Not only was it unusual for a man to talk to a woman because of her low status, but this particular woman was a Samaritan, an ethnic group despised by Jews. Jesus asked for a drink from the well, showing her great respect. And then he told her about living water, displaying his compassion for her soul: "Those who drink the water I give will never be thirsty again. It becomes a fresh, bubbling spring within them, giving them eternal life" (4:14).

Third, in one of the most dramatic and tender stories in the life of Jesus, a woman who had been bleeding for 12 years (and likely disowned by her family because she was "unclean") pressed through a large crowd and touched the hem of his garment (Luke 8:43-48). At first Jesus wondered who touched him, for he felt "healing power" go out of him. When the woman timidly came forward, Jesus called her "daughter," and said her faith had made her well.

Truly, Jesus was the embodiment of what it means to show compassion to those we tend to avoid and despise. Jesus didn't hesitate to welcome and relate to the broken, the marginalized, and the outcasts of society. He gladly accepted the accusations of the religious leaders that he was "a friend of tax collectors and other sinners" (Luke 7:34).

In another dramatic episode, Jesus encountered a widow whose son had died. "When the Lord saw her, his heart overflowed with compassion" (Luke 7:13). Jesus then brought the widow's son back to life, causing this reaction from the crowd:

> They were all filled with awe and praised God. "A great prophet has appeared among us," they said. "God has come to help his people." This news about Jesus spread throughout Judea and the surrounding country (Luke 7:14-15 NIV).

Compassion Is at the Center of God's Heart

By showing such awe-inspiring compassion, Jesus revealed the compassionate heart of God. In the Old Testament, the prophet Isaiah recorded the very words of God, who expressed his displeasure when his people fasted for external appearance rather than to show compassion to others. After giving them a tongue-lashing over their hypocrisy, God told them what kind of fasting he wants:

> "Free those who are wrongly imprisoned;
>   lighten the burden of those who work for you.
> Let the oppressed go free,
>   and remove the chains that bind people.
> Share your food with the hungry,
>   and give shelter to the homeless.
> Give clothes to those who need them,
>   and do not hide from relatives who need your help."
>   (Isaiah 58:6-7)

During his three years of public ministry, Jesus demonstrated every one of these acts of compassion, and he called those who followed him to do the same. In a sermon near the end of his earthly ministry, Jesus gave a preview of how he will evaluate those who stand before him on the day of judgment, only he personalized it, making himself the recipient of compassion. Those who are blessed by the Father are invited to "inherit the Kingdom prepared for you from the creation of the world." They are the ones who showed compassion to Jesus in these ways:

> "I was hungry, and you fed me. I was thirsty, and you gave me a drink. I was a stranger, and you invited me into your home. I was naked, and you gave me clothing. I was sick, and you cared for me. I was in prison, and you visited me" (Matthew 25:35-36).

Not comprehending what Jesus meant, the righteous will answer him:

> "Lord, when did we ever see you hungry and feed you? Or thirsty and give you something to drink? Or a stranger and show you hospitality? Or naked and give you clothing? When did we ever see you sick or in prison and visit you?" (Matthew 25:37-39).

And Jesus will reply,

> "I tell you the truth, when you did it to one of the least of these my brothers and sisters, you were doing it to me!" (Matthew 25:40).

This is such a beautiful and sobering reality, one that we don't take seriously enough. But we need to because, as F.B. Meyer writes, "Jesus identifies himself with all who are weary and heavy laden, who are sorrowful and sinful, who have drifted into hospitals and prisons of the world."[9]

The Early Church Took This Seriously

Christians living in the first century took the compassion of Jesus and his admonition to "do it to the least of these" seriously:

> They sold their property and possessions and shared the money with those in need. They worshiped together at the Temple each day, met in homes for the Lord's Supper, and shared their meals with great joy and generosity—all the while praising God and enjoying the goodwill of all the people. And each day the Lord added to their fellowship those who were being saved (Acts 2:45-47).

This passage is often misinterpreted to imply that the early church was a forerunner of socialism or even Communism. That's not what happened. The believers didn't move into a communal living arrangement, and they weren't required to sell their property and possessions. Instead, they developed a strong sense of community and shared a common vision and purpose, which was to give to meet needs as they arose.

The commitment of the early Christians produced in them a new attitude about their property and possessions. No longer was their goal to accumulate wealth for themselves. Instead, they used their resources for the cause of Christ and for the care of his people. As Ray Johnston, founding pastor of Bayside Church in California, has observed, "The *good deeds* of these believers led to *good will* in the community, which opened the door to share the *good news*."[10]

Showing Compassion Proves Your Faith Is Genuine

While the Bible is clear that your salvation is the result of faith and not by anything you do (Ephesians 2:8-9), your compassion and generosity will prove that your faith is genuine and alive (James 2:26). Don't get us wrong. There's nothing you can do to make God love you any more than he already does, but the things you do in response to his commands will please God. Here's what James wrote in his letter to Jewish Christians in the first century:

> Pure and genuine religion in the sight of God the Father means caring for orphans and widows in their distress and refusing to let the world corrupt you (James 1:27).

Keep in mind that before they became Christians, the Jewish people were very religious. By that we mean they were focused on religious ritual. But that's not what James has in mind here. The word for "religion" in this verse is all about right living, not a system of beliefs.

The reference to "caring for orphans and widows in their distress" has to do with *conduct.* This is the compassion you show to the people of special concern to God. "Refusing to let the world corrupt you" has to do with *character.* When your character is in line with God's heart, your conduct will be in line with his purpose for you:

> "Learn to do good.
>   Seek justice.
>   Help the oppressed.
>   Defend the cause of orphans.
>   Fight for the rights of widows."
>   (Isaiah 1:17)

Where Do You Start?

You may feel overwhelmed and even intimidated by the difficult and daunting task of helping people in need. We both reside in California, where 30 percent of the homeless population of the entire country lives. A good friend of ours who lives near Los Angeles recently expressed a desire to help the homeless but didn't know where to begin. "There are so many, and they don't seem to want help," she said. "I just don't know what I can do." Maybe you can relate to her. Helping people who are desperate and hurting may seem beyond your ability.

We have two suggestions that may be useful. First, identify those organizations in your community that are offering help and providing much-needed services to hurting people—whether widowed, orphaned, food deprived, homeless, sick, or in prison. You can certainly donate to such nonprofits, and you can also volunteer. Second, don't overlook the good you can do for one person. Refuse to fall for the misguided notion that if you can't do something big, you shouldn't do anything at all. As Andy Stanley has said, "Do for one what you wish you could do for everyone."

Compassion for the Spiritually Needy

We've talked throughout this chapter about the physical needs of people, and how caring for "the least of these" shows your love for Jesus. There's another kind of compassion you need to think about, and that's compassion for those who have yet to begin a new life with Jesus. You know people who are far from God, and you also know people who are close but have never experienced the new birth of a life surrendered to Jesus. They may be in your family. They may be close friends. For sure they are your neighbors.

We know how concerned Jesus was for the physical needs of people. But he was even more concerned for their spiritual needs. When Jesus read from the Scriptures in the synagogue in his hometown of Nazareth, here is the passage he highlighted. Notice how it includes both spiritual and physical needs:

> "The Spirit of the LORD is upon me,
>   for he has anointed me to bring Good News to the poor.
> He has sent me to proclaim that captives will be released,
>   that the blind will see,
> that the oppressed will be set free,
>   and that the time of the LORD's favor has come."
>   (Luke 4:18-19)

By quoting this prophetic passage from the Book of Isaiah, Jesus declared his dual mission. He would literally restore sight to the blind, but he would also help those who are spiritually blind to see. He would set the oppressed free, and he would also bring freedom to those who are spiritually oppressed. As much physical healing as Jesus did during his earthly ministry, he came primarily "to seek and save those who are lost" (Luke 19:10).

May your compassion for others include their physical needs, but never lose sight of sharing the life-changing faith you have found in Jesus.

AN ESSENTIAL FOR NEW CHRISTIANS

Because of the great compassion God has shown to us, we have the responsibility to show compassion for others. Notice how Paul summarizes this relationship between the compassion of God, the sufferings of Jesus, and the privilege we have to bring comfort to others:

> All praise to God, the Father of our Lord Jesus Christ. God is our merciful Father and the source of all comfort. He comforts us in all our troubles so that we can comfort others. When they are troubled, we will be able to give them the same comfort God has given us. For the more we suffer for Christ, the more God will shower us with his comfort through Christ (2 Corinthians 1:3-5).

Q&A
WHY DOES GOD ALLOW SUFFERING?

Through this book we have been telling you how much God loves the world and how much he loves you. That's why a question like this is a difficult one to answer. For one thing, it concerns the issue of suffering itself, and why there's so much of it in the world. This wasn't the way it was supposed to be. God created a perfect world without sin and without suffering, but it was a world where choice existed. God could have created us without the capability of choosing or doing wrong, but what good would that have been? God wants us to love him because we want to, not because we're forced to love him. In fact, you could say that by creating the world that way, God was demonstrating his love.

Because humanity chose to disobey God, sin entered the world, and with it suffering and evil. That's the other part of the answer to this question. Because God is altogether holy, he is not capable of causing suffering, but he does allow it. While that may seem harsh, think of it this way. If God did not allow suffering and evil, he would have to destroy everything evil that causes suffering, including us! But out of his great love and mercy, God not only allows us to live, but he has given us a way to get back into a right relationship with him (Romans 5:6-11).

That's the good news! While we were still sinners, God reached out in love and sent Jesus to live with us, die for us, and to be resurrected as the example of what is waiting for us. Someday, Jesus will return to earth to gather those who have believed in him, so that they might forever be with him in a place with no more suffering, evil, and death. We will be at perfect and eternal peace with him.

Chapter 10

Help Others Love God

At the end of his crucifixion, Jesus was pronounced dead, and his body was removed from the cross. They buried his body in a tomb (like a shallow cave in the side of a hill). A boulder weighing several tons was placed over the entrance to the tomb. A unit of four to ten Roman soldiers was assigned to guard the tomb 24/7. They only got to 24/3. On the third day, the tomb was found empty, and Jesus was alive.

This is the guy who was pronounced dead and removed from the cross, then buried in the cemetery for three days. The word on the street was that he had risen from the dead. The Roman soldiers couldn't explain how the body vanished. (The Bible says that they fainted in terror when an angel rolled away the huge boulder to reveal an empty tomb.) The Jewish religious leaders gave the soldiers hush money, and they concocted a phony story that the disciples had stolen the Jesus-corpse to fake a resurrection. But it was a 100 percent legit come-back-alive resurrection.

The Bible says that after his resurrection Jesus met a couple of times with the disciples and once with a group of 500 of his followers. The Jesus-sightings culminated on the fortieth day after the resurrection for a "going home" celebration. Jesus had a clandestine rendezvous with the disciples who had been with him for the duration of his three-year ministry. They met on a hillside near Bethany, a little town a couple of miles from Jerusalem. This was the time and place of the "ascension," when Jesus was transported up in the air, through the clouds, and back to heaven.

This was the last that Jesus would see of those who were his closest cohorts. This was the moment for him to give what would be his famous last words. He spoke directly to those disciples, but what he says applies to all of the additional disciples who would follow in future years—like you. The Bible recites what Jesus said in two different passages. Read these verses as if Jesus was talking directly to you...because he was.

> Jesus came and told his disciples, "I have been given all authority in heaven and on earth. Therefore, go and make disciples of all the nations, baptizing them in the name of the Father and the Son and the Holy Spirit. Teach these new disciples to obey all the commands I have given you. And be sure of this: I am with you always, even to the end of the age" (Matthew 28:18-20).

> "You will receive power when the Holy Spirit comes upon you. And you will be my witnesses, telling people about me everywhere—in Jerusalem, throughout Judea, in Samaria, and to the ends of the earth" (Acts 1:8).

As we discussed in chapter 7, this command given by Jesus to the disciples then (and to all of us who follow in Christ's footsteps) is called "The Great Commission." This is a sacred assignment for us to disseminate the Good News of Jesus around the globe to all people. Christians refer to this as evangelism—spreading the gospel to other people who don't follow Jesus or maybe don't know anything about him.

Billy Graham was a famous evangelist who preached Jesus to more than 200 million people. God probably isn't calling you to be Billy's replacement, and maybe not a missionary in the Sahara Desert, but Christ has called you to be an evangelist for him. If you are a new Christian, or even a longtime one, this may seem like an intimidating role to assume. But Jesus expects that you will develop a natural pattern in your life to talk about him to other people, some of whom will become disciples of Jesus like you, and some of whom won't.

> "Don't worry about how to defend yourself or what
> to say, for the Holy Spirit will teach you at that time
> what needs to be said" (Luke 12:11-12).

Unpacking the Great Commission

Think about this for a moment. The Almighty Creator of the universe has recruited you to join him in building his kingdom. What an honor. What a responsibility. It is simply incredible. And although it might not seem like it now, God will show you that it is incredibly simple. Just tell people what you know about Jesus. Here's a breakdown of the components of this commission Jesus gave to his disciples:

Jesus has been given all authority in heaven and earth. Jesus has disciples all around the earth. They are his ambassadors. You are one of them. Wherever you are, you are working on assignment for the One who has sovereign control of everything on earth and in heaven.

You are one of his witnesses. In the courtroom, a witness is a person who testifies. The judge and jury don't usually care about the witness's opinion, just the facts of what the witness has seen, heard, and experienced. That's all that God asks of you when you testify on his behalf. The testimony of a Christian is a simple retelling of what God has done in the Christian's life. No seminary degree in theology is required. Just tell your story.

You are to make disciples of Christ. Introduce people to Jesus Christ and you lead them on the path to accepting Jesus. You don't "make" disciples in the sense of saving them; Jesus does the saving. But you can get the process started. Maybe like someone did for you.

From all nations. Jesus was a Jew, but his salvation extends to Jews and non-Jews alike. As it says in John 3:16—God loves all people in the world. God may have some worldwide ministry in your future, but for right now it is certain that your mission field is the city where you live and the places where you hang out.

Baptizing them. Jesus is not in it for the head count. For him, it is not about the numbers. It is about transforming lives in those who are fully devoted to him. Jesus wants followers who absorb this teaching and have such an allegiance to him that they are willing to publicly proclaim that commitment in the ceremony of baptism.

In the name of the Father, Son, and Holy Spirit. Humility exists among the members of the Trinity. Jesus wants his followers to understand how this three-in-one God thing works so that his followers will have appreciation for the respective roles of the Father, Son, and Holy Spirit working in their lives.

Teaching them to obey his commands. Following Christ is not a matter of getting a free ticket to heaven. Accepting Christ is a commitment that includes submission to his will.

He is with you until he returns. You are not in this by yourself. God is with you, and he equips you.

Here's the problem: People don't know about Jesus. They need someone to tell them. Someone who actually knows Jesus. Someone like you.

> How can they call on him to save them unless they believe in him? And how can they believe in him if they have never heard about him? And how can they hear about him unless someone tells them? And how will anyone go and tell them without being sent? That is why the Scriptures say, "How beautiful are the feet of messengers who bring good news!" (Romans 10:14-15).

Communicating your God story is your testimony. It comes across in two ways. You can say it. And you can show it.

Say What You Know of Jesus

Some of those first Christians who lived in the areas of Jerusalem and Galilee in the years of AD 30–33 were privileged to see Jesus and hear him teach. They could give a testimony of one who was an eyewitness.

> We proclaim to you the one who existed from the beginning, whom we have heard and seen. We saw

> him with our own eyes and touched him with our
> own hands. He is the Word of life. This one who is
> life itself was revealed to us, and we have seen him.
> And now we testify and proclaim to you that he is
> the one who is eternal life. He was with the Father,
> and then he was revealed to us. We proclaim to you
> what we ourselves have actually seen and heard so
> that you may have fellowship with us. And our fel-
> lowship is with the Father and with his Son, Jesus
> Christ. We are writing these things so that you may
> fully share our joy (1 John 1:1-4).

Your experience will be a little different, but no less impactful. You have faith to believe in Jesus, even though you have never seen him. You have personal firsthand knowledge of how he has worked in your life. Tell that story.

> If you openly declare that Jesus is Lord and believe
> in your heart that God raised him from the dead,
> you will be saved. For it is by believing in your
> heart that you are made right with God, and it is
> by openly declaring your faith that you are saved
> (Romans 10:9-10).

Show What You Know About Jesus

Saint Francis of Assisi was a devoted friar who lived in the thir-teenth century. He had an interesting take on witnessing for Christ: "Preach the gospel at all times, and if necessary, use words."

As a Christian, what you do may be more important than what you say. Your conduct will be scrutinized to see if you are practicing what you are preaching. Live your life as if Jesus was living in your life… because that is exactly what is happening.

> Do everything without complaining and arguing,
> so that no one can criticize you. Live clean, inno-
> cent lives as children of God, shining like bright
> lights in a world full of crooked and perverse peo-
> ple (Philippians 2:14-15).

If you are public with your commitment to Jesus as he expects you to be, you may attract some hostility. Be firm in your faith. You don't need to debate. Your testimony is your personal story. How you respond is important because you will want to display Christlike qualities. Exhibiting Christ in your response is in itself a genuine example of Christ being in you.

> You must worship Christ as Lord of your life. And if
> someone asks about your hope as a believer, always
> be ready to explain it. But do this in a gentle and
> respectful way (1 Peter 3:15-16).

You represent Christ in the part of the world where he has placed you. The people with whom you are connected—in your family, your work or school, and in your social circles—may have no other exposure to God than you. Some of them will be eager to know about God; some may be reluctant; others may be obstinate—all of which is out of your control.

> "Anyone who believes in God's Son has eternal life. Anyone who doesn't obey the Son will never experience eternal life but remains under God's angry judgment" (John 3:36).

Your role is not to judge them. You don't get bonus points if they become believers, and you don't get demerits if they reject Christ. God only asks that you tell them the Good News of his love for them.

> Live wisely among those who are not believers, and make the most of every opportunity. Let your conversation be gracious and attractive so that you will have the right response for everyone (Colossians 4:5-6).

AN ESSENTIAL FOR NEW CHRISTIANS

Whether they are family members, friends, or strangers, God wants you to love others to the extent that you do not want them to go through life without realizing, understanding, and accepting the deep love God has for them. And if that's not enough motivation for you to tell others about Jesus, we'll put it a little more bluntly: You should love them too much to see them separated from the love of God for eternity in hell.

Jesus didn't come into the world to judge the world but to save the world. He demonstrated his love for us by laying down his life for us so that we could be saved. The least we can do is to tell our family, friends, and neighbors about the greatest love in the world.

You might think that this is an assignment that is outside your comfort level and beyond your capabilities. You are correct. This is a big deal. It is huge. So, never forget that God has equipped you with his Holy Spirit. Rely on that supernatural power as you share Christ's love.

Q&A
WHAT ABOUT SPIRITUAL WARFARE?

The Bible says that spiritual warfare is a real deal. There is a cosmic battle between the forces of God and his angels versus Satan and his demons.

> Be strong in the Lord and in his mighty power. Put on all of God's armor so that you will be able to stand firm against all strategies of the devil. For we are not fighting against flesh-and-blood enemies, but against evil rulers and authorities of the unseen world, against mighty powers in this dark world, and against evil spirits in the heavenly places (Ephesians 6:10-12).

Christians are smack dab in the middle of the battlefield. The eternal outcome is already known to both sides. When the timing is right according to God's timetable, Satan and his demons will be defeated and thrown into the lake of fire where they will be tormented for eternity.

Nonetheless, Satan and his demons want to oppose and obstruct God's purposes. They don't bother the non-Christians, most of whom unknowingly support and further Satan's strategies. And Satan can leave lukewarm Christians alone because they aren't doing anything to advance God's kingdom.

If you are a fully devoted follower of Christ, then Satan has you on his hit list. But fear not. Remember that while God and Satan are opposites, they are not equal opposites. This is a supernatural, cosmic mismatch that is fully under God's control. Don't get distracted by looking at the enemy; keep your eyes fixed on God.

> Let us run with endurance the race God has set
> before us. We do this by keeping our eyes on Jesus,
> the champion who initiates and perfects our faith
> (Hebrews 12:1-2).

God is with you and has equipped you for the battle.

> Therefore, put on every piece of God's armor so you
> will be able to resist the enemy in the time of evil.
> Then after the battle you will still be standing firm
> (Ephesians 6:13).

A Personal Note from the Authors

We don't know you. We don't know your name. We couldn't pick you out in a lineup. But we are praying for you. We are praying that these ten essentials will flourish in your life as you discover that God's love for you is limitless beyond human comprehension. As you will discover, these essentials are not only for new Christians, they are for all Christians at all times.

We are praying that you will quickly realize, if you haven't already, that being a follower of Christ is not about rules, regulations, or meaningless rituals. It is the opposite of all that. The essence of Christianity is about you having an intimate relationship with Jesus.

A non-Christian might say, "Oh, for the love of God!" as a substitute for swear words in a moment of frustration. It is our prayer for you that referring to "the love of God" will work its way into your daily conversations with reciprocal meanings:

- as an expression of *your love for God*, which governs your thoughts, your actions, and your conversations; and
- as an expression of *the love God showers on you* through his extravagant mercy and grace.

We pray that the essentials of your Christian faith will help you realize that God is enthusiastically in love with you, and that in response, by your actions and conversations, you will reflect the love of Christ to others.

We aren't the only ones who have prayed for you. In John 17, you can read the prayer that Jesus uttered on the night before he was crucified. He was praying to his heavenly Father, and he was praying for his disciples…and that includes you, now that you are a disciple of Christ. He was praying that his disciples (including you) would experience the fullness of eternal life when he said, "This is the way to eternal life—to know you, the only true God, and Jesus Christ, the one you sent to earth" (John 17:3).

The bottom line: Get to know Jesus. The more you know of him, the more you will love him. It will be a journey for the remainder of your life on earth, and it will culminate when you are face to face with Jesus in heaven. We will see you there!

Stan Jantz
Bruce Bickel

Notes

1. C.S. Lewis, *The Weight of Glory* (Grand Rapids, MI: William B. Eerdmans, 1972), 15.

2. D.L. Moody, *Secret Power* (Chicago, IL: Revell, 1881), 46.

3. A.W. Tozer, *Discipleship* (Chicago, IL: Moody, 2018), 92.

4. F.B. Meyer, *F.B. Meyer Bible Commentary* (Wheaton, IL: Tyndale House, 1979), 408.

5. Richard Langer and Joanne J. Jung, *The Call to Follow* (Wheaton, IL: Crossway, 2022), 70.

6. Dallas Willard, *The Divine Conspiracy* (San Francisco, CA: HarperSanFrancisco, 1998), 283.

7. Bill Hull, *The Complete Book of Discipleship* (Colorado Springs, CO: NavPress, 2006), 214.

8. Bill Hull, *The Complete Book of Discipleship* (Colorado Springs, CO: NavPress, 2006), 234-236.

9. F.B. Meyer, *F.B. Meyer Bible Commentary* (Wheaton, IL: Tyndale House, 1979), 414.

10. Ray Johnston—heard in a live sermon, but the date of his message is unknown.